NIGHTINGALE-CONANT CORPORATION

THE POWER OF GOALS

SOUND WISDOM BOOKS
BY EARL NIGHTINGALE

The Strangest Secret

Lead the Field

The Direct Line

Successful Living in a Changing World

*Your Success Starts Here: Purpose
and Personal Initiative*

*Transformational Living: Positivity,
Mindset, and Persistence*

*Your Greatest Asset: Creative Vision
and Empowered Communication*

*Master Your Inner World: Overcome
Negative Emotions, Embrace Happiness,
and Maximize Your Potential*

THE STRANGEST SECRET SERIES

*30 Days to Self-Confidence: A Guide to Stop
Doubting Yourself and Start Succeeding*

*The Power of Goals: **Timeless Lessons on Finding
Purpose, Overcoming Doubt, and Taking Action***

What we're doing is keeping the main thing, the main thing.

—**ZIG ZIGLAR**,
GOALS

EARL NIGHTINGALE
THE POWER OF GOALS

Timeless Lessons on Finding Purpose,
Overcoming Doubt, and Taking Action

THE STRANGEST SECRET SERIES

© Copyright 2025– Nightingale-Conant Corporation

All rights reserved. This book is protected by the copyright laws of the United States of America. No part of this publication may be reproduced, stored in or introduced into a retrieval system, or transmitted, in any form or by any means (electronic, mechanical, photocopying, recording or otherwise), without the prior written permission of the publisher. For permissions requests, contact the publisher, addressed "Attention: Permissions Coordinator," at the address below.

Published and distributed by:
SOUND WISDOM
P.O. Box 310
Shippensburg, PA 17257-0310
717-530-2122

info@soundwisdom.com

www.soundwisdom.com

While efforts have been made to verify information contained in this publication, neither the author nor the publisher assumes any responsibility for errors, inaccuracies, or omissions. While this publication is chock-full of useful, practical information; it is not intended to be legal or accounting advice. All readers are advised to seek competent lawyers and accountants to follow laws and regulations that may apply to specific situations. The reader of this publication assumes responsibility for the use of the information. The author and publisher assume no responsibility or liability whatsoever on the behalf of the reader of this publication.

The scanning, uploading and distribution of this publication via the Internet or via any other means without the permission of the publisher is illegal and punishable by law. Please purchase only authorized editions and do not participate in or encourage piracy of copyrightable materials.

ISBN 13 TP: 978-1-64095-501-1

ISBN 13 eBook: 978-1-64095-502-8

For Worldwide Distribution, Printed in the U.S.A.

1 2024

Success is the progressive realization of a worthy ideal.

—EARL NIGHTINGALE

CONTENTS

INTRODUCTION

by Vic Conant

My dad, Lloyd Conant, met Earl Nightingale in 1956 when Earl was a popular radio commentator on WGN in Chicago. At the time, Dad was a successful businessman, he owned his own direct marketing and printing company. Earl had just produced a recording titled *The Strangest Secret* and was looking for someone to market that product. The two of them met and Dad ended up selling a million of that recording over the years. These two men were a match made in Heaven. My dad the marketer and Earl the talent.

Earl, like Lloyd, was a "Great Depression" era child and grew up poor in California. Earl educated himself; he was an avid reader and a brilliant guy. Both had only a high school education. Earl was a totally self-made man as was my dad, so the two of them hit it off and eventually created Nightingale-Conant when I was about 14.

Every individual who has discovered what Earl Nightingale calls *The Strangest Secret* throughout the ages has found it to be a profoundly life-changing discovery. That secret? *You become what you think about*—and the fact that our thoughts *control* and, many believe, *create* our reality. Consequently, there is great responsibility placed on our thinking, making us responsible for our own future.

Vic Conant
Chairman of the Board
Nightingale-Conant Corporation

1

TARGETS

*People with goals—goals they've set
their hearts and minds on—are always
moving toward achieving those goals.*

Even while we goal-oriented people sleep, our deep minds are apparently working on the project. That's why we often awake early in the morning with clearly in mind a solution to a problem that offered resistance to our progress.

We think about our goal as we have our morning coffee and breakfast. While we're in the shower, and it comes to us again and again during the day. We are on course. We're moving toward the fulfillment of our current goal, and it's often the last thing we think about as we drop off to sleep. It's our aiming point, our target, and people with aiming points tend to reach them.

It's astonishing how people with goals tend to live longer than people without them. It's as though they can extend their lives simply because they still have something to do. It's the interest that seems to lend vitality and energy to

People with goals tend to live longer.

their lives. And when they do come to the end of their lives, they're caught up in full stride, fully alive, and still moving toward a new and interesting port of call.

An old ship has successfully visited thousands of ports of call. There have been storms, and breakdowns, delays when they've had to anchor offshore for a while, but the life of the ship has been one of one success after another.

That old ship analogy is the way goal-oriented people spend their lives. Each goal successfully reached finds them better equipped and with more experience to set the next one. Goals for such people tend to ascend in stair-like fashion, each one a bit more demanding and fulfilling than the one before. In a few years, they find themselves accomplishing with surprising ease goals that would've been impossible when they began their gyrate into the future.

Cervantes, author of *Don Quixote,* wrote, "The journey is better than the inn." The journey toward the meaningful goals of our lives leads us into new areas of interest and the most surprising kinds of *synchronicity*—which we won't find sitting still in the "inn." Quite often, if we read a story with the kind of coincidences that are often a natural part of a goal-oriented person's active life, we'd put it down while muttering, "Impossible."

But astonishing as it may seem, that kind of synchronicity becomes an active part of the goal-oriented person's life. The right people seem to show up at just the right time. Situations suddenly change, opening, yawning chasms of opportunity where before there were none. At a meeting, we find ourselves being introduced to the exact person we most need at that particular stage of our journey. A minor accident, which we may at first see as a setback, turns out to be a blessing in disguise.

For the people working toward goals, it sometimes seems as though the smiling face of good fortune has joined us on our quest, and we should learn to be alert for such serendipitous occurrences. They're part of being on the journey rather than resting in the inn.

We should not try to force such happenings. We must learn, as the Daoist reminds us, not to push the river. We need to go with the flow. The right things will happen at the right time without forcing, without impatience. If we keep steadily on course, our goal clearly in mind, success is inevitable.

Thoughts to Think About

1   How familiar with the word "synchronicity"
     are you? If unfamiliar, you are encouraged to
     do some deep-diving research. Keep in mind
     what you find as you read through this book.

2.   Do you consider yourself a goal-oriented person?
     If not, what type of "oriented" person are you
     when it comes to your life's perspective?

3.   Do you believe that most if not all goal-
     oriented people live longer?

Notes:

_____

_____

_____

_____

_____

_____

_____

_____

_____

_____

_____

2

GOAL-ORIENTED PEOPLE

Successful people are those who discover that life is quite ready and willing to meet their requirements. They set their incomes to meet their needs and wants through discovering within themselves a marketable factor and developing that factor to whatever degree necessary in order to derive the appropriate reward response.

Unsuccessful people may be said to be those who make their lifestyles fit. Whatever wages they receive, they put themselves on the receiving end of things and have little to say about their own welfare. Successful people put themselves behind the wheel of their lives. The unsuccessful ride in the passenger seats.

Almost everything has an economic base today, at least for more than half the human population. We're usually rewarded by the amount of money we receive for what we do in a free society. And what we charge for what we do in a free society are largely matters of personal choice.

*You earn your rewards
through time and experience.*

If we find our best interests and opportunities for personal expression within the framework of a large corporation, we can so develop and apply ourselves as to reach whatever levels of accomplishment and reward we're willing to earn. It takes time to succeed, and it should. We need seasoning for the success we decide to achieve. We need to earn our rewards through the daily passage of time and experience so that each successive step is accepted and applauded by those who have come to know us.

Meaningful and richly rewarding journeys take time. They take preparation and careful planning. And as every seasoned traveler knows, they're subject to the vagaries of incidents and the mistakes and inefficiencies of others along the way. But the journey has its adventures and misadventures, and it has a definite upward momentum—there's no doubting its eventual destination, for that is the goal of the person in command.

Each new upward step along the way prepares our resolute traveler for the next plateau. And if he or she doesn't lose the exciting vision of the goal to be reached or meet with an untimely end—the silent tragedy of war and accident—the goal with all the trimmings will be reached.

The journey is your life, our holiday on earth, your time here as you successively set new goals or dive back into your great river of interest—or both. You receive what you fully expect to receive and usually a good deal more. *You become what you think about.*

You become successful to the extent of your true desires and determination, and you do so by building on your strong point, at what you do best, what gives you the most, the deepest satisfaction. Whatever that is, it can be honed to marketable proportions in some way and applied in service to others to earn you the rewards you seek, and should have and will have. That's your part of the process of success.

No one's supposed to do that for you, or hold your hand, or rush to your aid every time you slip or fall back a little. That's the earning part that falls on us and prepares each of us for the future. There's help enough on every side if we're wise enough and energetic enough to make use of it, help in the form of books, recorded programs, skills to hone,

You become successful according to your true desires and determination.

and the numerous people who do come to our aid once we're on course. But such people need not be sought nor importuned. They come of their own natural need, at just the right time. Events begin to fall into our lives like missing pieces of a jigsaw puzzle. They're the mark of people with the attitude that tells the world they know where they are going and fully expect to get there.

We all know the stories of Alexander Graham Bell and Thomas Edison; the businesses that have grown from their inventions circle the globe and are among the largest on the planet. Einstein was such a person, of course, but there are thousands of them we never hear of. There are people who would be perfectly content in their fields of interest with only a modest maintenance diet and a roof over their heads. Their work is everything.

In the best instances, the person and the job fit together and belong together perfectly, like a key in a lock. I believe that each of us, because of the way our genetic heritage is stacked, has an area of great interest. And it's that area that we should explore with a patience and diligence of a paleontologist in an important dig, for it's a region of great potential. Somewhere within it, we can find that avenue of interest that so perfectly matches our natural abilities. We'll be able to make our greatest contribution and spend our lives in work we love.

If we can find our river of interest, we need only throw ourselves into it fully committed and there spend our days learning, and growing, and finding new emerging

We should explore our area of interest with the patience and diligence of a paleontologist in an important dig, for it is a region of great potential.

Goals give you drive, direction, motivation, and energy.

fields of interest within its boundaries. If we cannot, then it's incumbent upon us to find our greatest aptitudes and employ them in whatever field offers us the greatest challenge and opportunity. Then we need only set goals to reach.

Many may ask, "Why set goals at all? Why not just take things as they come and do your best with what you have with which to work?" **A goal paints a picture for the subconscious.** Without a goal, we're much like the person with a boat and nowhere to go. Goals give us the drive and energy. We need to remain on the track long enough for their accomplishment. Goals motivate us. Like the captain of a ship about to leave port, we should be able to tell anyone our next port of call. If you've done much traveling at sea, you are perhaps surprised in the beginning by how slowly most large ships move through the water.

In a time when it's common for us to drive in our vehicles at 60 and 70 miles an hour and fly at 600 miles an hour, a ship pulling away from the dock and heading for a distant port at 20 knots may seem slow indeed—but the ship moves steadily 24 hours a day, always on course. One day, we rise to see the distant shore, and soon we're in the harbor with mission accomplished.

Now, the ship must have a new destination.

Thoughts to Think About

1. Never have the opportunities for us been so great. But the vast majority of people will be the beneficiaries of progress, not those who bring it about. Which group do you belong to?

2. Are you behind the wheel, driving toward the accomplishment of your life's goal? Or are you riding in the passenger seat, just going along for the ride, day after day after day?

3. What picture have you painted for your subconscious that reflects your goals? Describe it.

Notes:

_____

_____

_____

_____

_____

_____

_____

_____

_____

_____

3

FLEXIBLE EQUILIBRIUM

Throughout our history, America has produced a long list of "goal people" who made life better for the beneficiaries of good ideas. Beginning in 1728, one visionary published a host of America's very first self-help books, newspapers, pamphlets, and almanacs. Titles include *The Art of Making Money, The Way to Wealth, Every Man His Own Doctor,* and *Poor Richard's Almanac.* The author's name of this last work was Richard Saunders, but that was a pseudonym for the publisher, Benjamin Franklin.

One of the greatest men the world has produced was our own Benjamin Franklin—a man of amazing genius and everybody should read his autobiography. It's a great inspirational book and a book which if followed, would bring all the success anyone could hope for in life.

As Carl Van Doren wrote about him in the book that earned him a Pulitzer Prize, "In any age, in any place, Franklin would've been great. Mind and will, talent and art, strength and ease, wit and grace met in him as if nature had been lavish and happy when he was shaped."[1]

Nothing seems to have been left out of Benjamin Franklin's makeup except a passionate desire as in most men of genius to be all ruler, all soldier, all saint, all poet, all scholar, all one gift or merit or success. Franklin's powers were from first to last in a flexible equilibrium. Even his genius could not specialize him; he moved through his world in a humorous mastery of it. He seems to have been more than any single man, a harmonious human multitude. Yes, Benjamin Franklin was about 20 outstanding men all combined in the form of one.

One of the things he's best remembered for was his advice on the importance of thrift in all things. He said, "Waste neither time nor money, but make the best use of both." And to give you an idea of how he lived up to his own advice, he left at his death a thousand pounds, that's about $5,000, each to the cities of Boston and Philadelphia. This money was not to be touched for 200 years except part of it, which could be used for some good public work after 100 years. You see, Franklin knew that the best invention was compound interest.

He died in the year 1790, which means the money may be used by the cities of Boston, where he was born, and Philadelphia, where he lived and worked, in the year 1991, 200 years after his death. Do you have any idea how much a thousand pounds sterling or about $5,000 will grow to with

---

1. Carl Van Doren, *Benjamin Franklin* (New York: Penguin Books, 1991).

compound interest in 200 years? Well, authorities estimate that Franklin's original 1,000 pounds will have grown by the year 1991 to $3,500,000.

The hand of Benjamin Franklin will reach out of the grave and give to the people of two cities about three and a half million dollars each, or a total of $7 million. If anybody wants some advice on how to be a printer, publisher, writer, philosopher, diplomat, statesman, city engineer, president, or inventor—he invented all kinds of things. This is the guy to study, Benjamin Franklin, a goal-oriented man.

If you have youngsters you want to get started on the right track, have them read Benjamin Franklin's autobiography; and if you haven't read it yourself, I strongly encourage you to do so. It's interesting and exciting reading about the most important period in our country's life and certainly by one of the most important founders. He arrived in Philadelphia penniless with only a loaf of bread under his arm—and he helped write our Constitution and was one of its signers.

Waste neither time nor money, but make the best use of both.

Thoughts to Think About

1. How would you define the phrase "flexible equilibrium" as it relates to your current lifestyle?

2. How does flexible equilibrium applied to Franklin defy the phrase "jack of all trades, master of none"?

3. Will you make it a point to read Franklin's autobiography? What do you plan to gain from learning more about him?

Notes:

_____

_____

_____

_____

_____

_____

_____

_____

_____

_____

_____

_____

_____

4

GOOD ENOUGH-ERS

As society moves ahead, it seems that these days its inadequacy compounds. Like small children in a department store, they're not tall enough to see the brilliant displays of products, which we might call opportunities, nor mature enough to afford to buy them or qualify for them. They wander through life making minimum contributions and reaping minimum rewards as a consequence.

That so many of these childlike adults can live so well in the United States is a testimony to the viability of this abundant and productive free market economy and private enterprise system. They're not successful people. They're simply beneficiaries of the system.

In most other countries, they'd be much worse off than they are here. They are the "that's good enough-ers." They've done no more than absolutely necessary for survival for as long as they've participated, beginning in elementary school. If a passing grade will do in most of the subjects, they will, with the help of an overly lenient school system, find themselves with millions of other children pushed and pulled along until they reach an age when they can quit school altogether or perhaps graduate from high school.

They don't ask themselves, *How can I make my greatest contribution to society?* in the understanding that their rewards can never exceed their service. None approach a prospective employer with the idea of improving the business. They don't think in terms of the company's profit or loss. Instead, it's "What can I get out of this?" They have the whole thing backward, and they go through life that way. Backward.

Perhaps from time to time they wonder why they remain at the bottom of the pile, but an understanding of how the system works is as foreign to such people as the language of the Tierra del Fuegians or the inner workings of the New York Stock Exchange. Most amazing of all is the total absence of the understanding of how a very good and satisfactory income is achieved. Yes, it's a matter of lack of education, but it's also a lack of understanding fundamental economics.

There is also the complete misunderstanding of the very real fact that work can be interesting and enjoyable, challenging and wonderfully rewarding from a psychological as well as financial standpoint. It's quite possible to understand all of this and succeed dramatically as someone without a formal education. Millions of well-to-do Americans have very little real formal education.

What you do to qualify for life, liberty, and the pursuit of happiness is strictly up to you.

That beautiful statement in the Bill of Rights, that all men are created equal, that they're endowed by their Creator with certain unalienable rights, is a political statement. It guarantees life, liberty, and the pursuit of happiness to all people who are citizens of this favored land. But while their rights are guaranteed, the rest must be up to them. What they do to qualify themselves for life, liberty, and the pursuit of happiness is strictly up to each person.

Happily, learning what we need to know to move into the upper echelons of education and reward is not all that difficult. It takes a certain amount of dedication and discipline, which unfortunately for many is looked upon as an invasion of those very liberties in the pursuit of happiness the Bill of Rights tells us about. Each person has the choice to be dedicated and accept discipline to succeed. Sound economics is at the bottom of everything desirable. There must be a satisfactory financial base for our lives if we're to grow and accomplish more and experience more. Money is very important. Without it, nothing happens. With it, everything becomes possible.

For example, Warren Buffett—one of the top ten richest people in the world—got started selling newspapers when he was a boy. It's amazing how many of today's billionaires started as kids with an entrepreneurial spirit. Another example, Mark Cuban of *Shark Tank* is worth more than $6 billion and he started as a kid selling garbage bags door to door.

Let me give you another example. A 16-year-old boy during vacation finds that he needs some money. He begins to think about it, and all of a sudden an idea pops into his mind. He sits down and writes a little note on about a hundred pieces of paper. The note reads, "Student. Will wash and wax your car. Excellent job guaranteed. Call _____ " and he writes in his telephone number.

Then he goes to the nearest large shopping center and puts these little messages on the windshields of 100 cars. During the next few days, he receives 10 calls. He washes and waxes 10 cars for $10 each, resulting in making $100, less the cost of his supplies. Let's say he shows a net profit of $75. Now he has $75, the result of earning the needed money. Because he wanted money, it forced him to get an idea, and the idea got him the money he needed—but the idea was free.

Now the difference between this story and a man who builds a million-dollar business is only one of degree. The man who gets an idea to get a certain job, the earnings of which permit him to marry and support a family, can give all the credit for his earnings to the fact that he got the idea to learn that particular line of work.

Money-making ideas are free!

In other words, the money someone earns during their lifetime is all profit, the result of an idea—and ideas are free. Because of this, the human mind is the greatest profit-maker in the world. Ideas come to us, the best ones, as the result of an emotion, a strong feeling about something. The high school boy felt strongly about his need for some money. The millionaire is driven by strong emotional feelings.

Brain surgeons link emotions with imagination. Their knives are proving that every brain has a section that can create ideas. It's called the silent area, since it controls no body movement and has nothing to do with what we see or hear or physically feel. Back of this area is a lump of tissue called the thalamus. In this lobe, our basic emotions are centered, so our emotional center of the brain is next to this silent area, from which it is believed ideas are created.[2]

This means that you can get ideas to solve your emotional needs. You can actually create ideas. This gives each

2. Daniel Salzman, MD, PhD, "The Ties that Bind: Brain Cells Link Emotion with the Sensory World," *Columbia University, Zuckerman Institute*, July 2, 2015; https://zuckermaninstitute.columbia.edu/ties-bind-brain-cells-link-emotion-sensory-world; accessed January 19, 2024.

human being an enormous amount of power and control over the future—for while ideas are free and not limited in number, one idea can get you anything you want.

Thoughts to Think About

1. Are you now or have you been in the past a "good enough-er"? How did you, or how will you emerge from that mindset to grab more gusto and success in life?

2. Do you lack a basic understanding of fundamental economics? Do you believe that work can be interesting and enjoyable, challenging and wonderfully rewarding from a psychological as well as financial standpoint?

3. What steps will you take to actively pursue and earn a good life, appreciate daily liberty, and enjoy a lifetime of happiness?

Notes:

_____

_____

_____

_____

_____

_____

_____

_____

_____

5

A PERFECT-BALANCE LIFESTYLE

Know what you want.

There is something important in the world for each of us to do, and in order to do it well, we can't be in too much of a hurry. Youth is a time of confusion and impatience, of fear and doubt. Doubt as to what course we should follow and doubt as to our ability to get on well in the world. What should people shoot for, young and old alike, who still haven't found their place in life? What is a goal worth striving toward? I believe it can be summed up in one word—balance.

For example, try in your mind's eye, try to imagine a person who lives in perfect balance. Now to me, it conjures up a picture of a person of quiet serenity with courage. This person is employed in work he loves and does this work in a masterful way. He's a kind and loving parent. Quick to laugh, quick to smile and compliment others, slow to criticize. He's aware of his powers and of his ignorance. He has found his world, and he fills it with competence and good cheer. Being in the place that is right for him, he's found the area of his greatest strength. It's not necessarily a physical strength by any means, but strength of character, strength of purpose, and the quiet strength that brings comfort and security to his loved ones.

This to me is a goal worth working toward. It's the kind of mental picture that tends to clear away the confusion, the impatience, the fear and doubt. There is such a place for every person. Just knowing that such a world exists for us, if we find it, can keep us from straying off the track leading to success.

Too many people look at a job from the standpoint of how much money they will bring home. This is the wrong perspective because what looks like a lot of money at 18 or 20 or at even 25 might look like far too little at 45.

There's no such thing as a good job unless the job is right and satisfying for the person doing it. The first considerations should be, "Is this work I love or I like? Is this work I'm willing to devote the rest of my working career to over the next 40 years?" If it's the right work or leading

The only good job is one that satisfies you.

into the right field, the money will take care of itself. If it's the wrong field, all the money in the world won't make it right.

With a goal of achieving a perfectly balanced lifestyle and knowing that it can be achieved, you can begin to confidently look for your place in life. As Emerson put it in his classic book *Self-Reliance*, "Do that which is assigned you, and you cannot hope too much or dare too much." A man should learn to detect and watch that gleam of light that flashes across his mind from within more than the luster of the firmament of bards and sages. Yet he dismisses without notice his thought because it's his. It seems that the people who are most dissatisfied with their lives are those who tried to play it safe and easy.

Remember, life is a journey. Don't get off at the first stop unless you're sure it's where you want to live. There's more, much more up ahead.

Similarities of Success

How do you discover the right opportunities? One way is to look into the most interesting, small, and almost invisible differences that exist between someone who goes to the top and one who does not. There's no single formula that you can put your finger on except *desire and knowing where you're going*. Some of the top people in business and industry are graduates of our finest schools with top grades and near-perfect scholastic records, men and women from fine old families. But some of the highest-paid executives came from poor and broken homes, worked their way through the mills and mines and farms and had dirty fingernails for many years before they breathed the controlled, filtered air of the top executive suites. But they all had a few things in common, so let's look not at their differences but their similarities.

For one thing, all these goal-oriented people had the tiny inextinguishable spark of *desire*. It may have been money at first, but not always, and it always winds up as a *desire for achievement*, not money, achievement. These people have never been satisfied with what they have accomplished, no matter how great their accomplishments may seem to others. They all realized that they couldn't stop and coast, that they're either growing or dying in the business world. There's just no such thing as sitting back and saying, "Well, we're in. Now we can just relax." There've been a lot of companies, and some of them giants at one time or another, that have made this mistake and they're no longer around at all.

Goal-oriented people have an inextinguishable spark of desire.

Those at the top also have in common a *dissatisfaction with things as they are*. They know the truth of the saying that if it works, it's obsolete.

Another important commonality is the *ability and the personal incentive to work long hours*. To get to the top, you have to live your job. It has to be so challenging and interesting that it completely fills your life. You may take the family to the movies or out for dinner, but all the way to and all the way home, your mind is on your business. You go to bed thinking about it and you wake up *thinking* about it, *not worrying* about it. That's something else, and worrying comes true from time to time. But thinking about it constantly.

Thoughts to Think About

1. In your mind's eye, imagine a person who lives in perfect balance. Write what you see.

2. Are you leading a perfectly balanced lifestyle? What area(s) are out of balance? Financial? Marital? Physical? Emotional? Relational?

3. What is the strongest desire you have right now that is affecting your balance?

Notes:

_____

_____

_____

_____

_____

_____

_____

_____

_____

_____

_____

_____

_____

_____

6

OPPORTUNITY LURKS EVERYWHERE

Your dreams point to your desires.

I discovered a way to know what you really want—watch and pay attention to your dreams, your sleeping dreams and your daydreams. In them, you can generally find a clue to your unfulfilled desires. The reason I bring this up is because of the number of people who say they don't know what they want—so I tell them to pay attention to their dreams.

Daydreams like night dreams are usually about unsatisfied desires and they serve a very valuable purpose. They act as safety valves in many cases and actually keep people from going off the deep end. Instead of daydreaming about what is actually happening, in night dreams, people keep honest by projecting themselves into the unpredictable future and dream that this is going to happen.

Everybody daydreams; and believe it or not, everybody dreams at night. Some experts say that it's as impossible to sleep without dreaming as it would be to sleep without breathing. Some people say they don't dream. Maybe you don't think you dream, but that's because you don't remember what you dream about every time.

To prove that you dream every night and a way to remember what you dreamt about, which is valuable in determining what you really want, is just before you go to sleep, concentrate on remembering when you wake up the next morning, everything you dream about during the night. Keep a pad of paper and a pen on your bedside table, and the moment you wake up, try to remember your dreams. You'll be pleasantly surprised at how easy it is once you get the hang of it.

And about your daydreams, try to pin down a recurring daydream and analyze why you keep thinking about it. Maybe a dream is trying to tell you something. You'd be amazed at the number of successful men and women who are daily engaged in turning their daydreams into reality, literally making their dreams come true.

Most of the world's greatest accomplishments have been achieved by those who first dreamed of doing them

*Turn your dreams into reality—
make your dreams come true!*

and followed through. If you know how to go about it, you can turn your daydreams into actual realities. So the next time you find yourself daydreaming, grab hold of that dream and examine it. Maybe it's something you should pursue. Our dreams, daydreams and night dreams, are part of us. Many of them are silly and impractical and they'll be quickly forgotten. But maybe lurking somewhere in there is the one that's trying to tell us that it's worth coming true.

In an issue of *Good Business* magazine, I ran across an interesting copy of an Eric Butterworth broadcast. Let me quote from it:

> A little boy was leading his sister up a mountain path and she complained, "Why it's not a path at all, it's all rocky and bumpy." "Sure," he said, "the bumps are what you climb on." Life for each of us has its seeming defeats and frustrations. No one ever bats a thousand. No one wins in every encounter, but the really interesting thing is the way in which even bad breaks or terrible mistakes can and often do lead to unexpected blessings with the help of course of a little resilience and resourcefulness.
>
> A boy in Decatur, Illinois, was deeply interested in photography. He answered an ad in a magazine ordering a book on photography. Well, the publishers made a mistake and sent him instead a book about magic and

ventriloquism. The young lad was fascinated with the section on ventriloquism and he began practicing the art of throwing his voice. He created a wooden dummy to whom at one time millions of people listened on Sunday evenings, Charlie McCarthy. Edgar Bergen had turned a mistake into a fabulous career.

In your own frustrating experience, Eric Butterworth went on to say that "You can and should take a good look at a bad break. There may well be in your frustration, the means of making it fruitful." Whistler, the renowned artist, wanted more than anything to be a soldier. He even entered West Point as a cadet, but he failed a chemistry examination. Later he joked about the one wrong answer that meant the difference between passing and failing. He said, "If silicon had been a guess, I would've been a major general instead of an artist." These are prime examples of synchronicity!

The Joy of Synchronicity

Perhaps the reason for our sense of frustration in life is that we lose sight of our objective. We forget that the purpose of life is growth and development. We forget that there's probably something extremely helpful to us even in the reverse, a challenge to discover and release our greater potential.

High up in the north of Scotland, there's a hunting lodge, which has become a famous showplace. One day many years ago, an inebriated guest opened a bottle of soda and sprayed the contents over the newly decorated wall. It left an unsightly splotch stretching from floor to ceiling. The guests went away feeling that the displeasure of their host was justified, but one man remained behind. He studied the blotch on the wall, and then he went to work on it with crayons and charcoal, and finally with oil paints. He turned the brown stains into brown highland rocks with a cascade pouring over them.

Where the stain had been deepest, he painted a high-land stag leaping into the torrent, pursued by hunters in the background. Thus did Sir Edwin Landseer, the great artist, create a beautiful mural, bringing good out of evil, beauty out of ugliness. Now, visitors come from near and far to see Landseer's picture. Perhaps the blunders of our lives could be transformed after all into beauty, challenge, growth, and fulfillment. Again and again, we learn the truth that it isn't what happens *to* us that matters so much as it is our *reaction* to what happens that makes the real difference. Opportunity lurks everywhere.

Know What You Want

The facts are that most people don't know what they want. In fact, if a genie appeared before them and offered to grant them anything they wanted, they couldn't tell him what's most important to them. The trouble with people is not in achieving their goals, but in establishing them and staying with them until they've been won. Statistics prove that most people are waiting. They can't tell you what they're waiting for, but they're waiting all the same. They're hoping that, "Oh, something good will happen to me, or at least that nothing bad will." In the meantime, they're content to just wait and go along with whatever comes along.

It's also a fact that not one working person in a hundred realizes that the job he now has holds more opportunity in it than he could develop in a lifetime. If you think about it and give it the care and attention it deserves and you deserve. Nobody is supposed to tell you how to be successful in your company or industry. You're supposed to figure that out for

Your current job holds more opportunity in it than you can develop in a lifetime.

yourself by learning all you can, by doing all you can, and by becoming a professional at what it has been given you to do.

You'd be surprised at the number of people who think they should just automatically advance in their company whether they do anything to earn it or not, and that they should just automatically get pay raises whether they make themselves more valuable or not. These are the uninformed who feel that just being alive and present is enough, and they're to be pitied because they miss out on so much enjoyment, so much satisfaction and reward that could be theirs if they would just get out of their own way and do something.

Above all, decide what you want. That's the key. Anybody who feels they aren't getting anywhere should ask themselves: *What do I want?* and *Were do I want to go?* and *What am I doing to reach that goal?* If you can answer those questions positively, you're a success.

Thoughts to Think About

1. Are you a dreamer? How many dreams on average do you have each night? Each day? Do any come to mind that you may want to make a reality?

2. Thinking back, write a few examples of when synchronicity showed up in your life.

3. Would your friends and/or family label you a "sit and wait-er" or a "up and at-em" person most of the time?

Notes:

_____

_____

_____

_____

_____

_____

_____

_____

_____

_____

_____

_____

7

A TRICKY QUESTION

I'm going to ask you a very tricky question. However, it's important that you answer it the moment you read it. I'm going to ask you a question that everyone should have given a lot of thought to and can answer immediately and in one sentence—but I might add that it's a question only a few people out of a thousand can answer. At any rate, get ready and let's see how well you do. Here comes the question: What do you want more than anything else in the world?

Time's up. Now the chances are you answered one of three things, health, wealth, or happiness. Of course, if you happen to have a particular problem at the moment, you may have thought of that, but let's take the three that statistics prove most people want health, wealth, and happiness.

About *number one, health,* that's a tricky one. It can depend on a lot of factors such as your parents, the state of your emotions, and so forth. We leave that one where it belongs in the hands of your common sense and a reputable doctor.

Number two, wealth. This can be earned through knowledge, a lot of thinking, a lot of hard work, and yes, anyone can solve this one if you make it your major goal in life and are willing to spend from 12 to 18 hours a day for a number of years earning it. All you have to do is make up your mind that's what you want, and then be willing to sacrifice just about anything for its achievement.

But now let's talk about *number three, happiness.* Here's where most people get fooled. Happiness cannot be sought directly as an end in itself or it will forever elude you. You see, happiness is not a cause, it's an effect. It always comes as a result of doing something well, and the experts say that it's not really happiness that we're after at all. It's *joy* and joy only comes from achievement. Let me give you an example. If you make a perfect golf shot to the green, it makes you happy, but the happiness game is a result of the perfect golf shot, so if you want to be happier on a golf course, give it a lot of practice so that you'll become a better golfer.

Theoretically, happiness on the course should follow, and it's the same with life. If you want to be happy or experience maximum joy from life, you have to become better at this business of living, and joy never comes from pure receiving.

Joy comes only from achievement, from giving.

Joy only comes from contributing or giving. If you think back, you will remember that you've been happiest and experienced the greatest joy right after you accomplished something really worthwhile. People frequently find the experience an emotional letdown, a feeling of uneasiness on a Sunday evening or Monday morning. It's because frequently on weekends we don't do very much. Crazy as it may sound, kids are usually happier during the school term than they are during summer vacation, although they'll never admit it.

Human beings need something worthwhile to do constantly or they start losing out in the happiness department. The next time you start feeling uneasy or depressed, dig into your work. You'll be surprised how many problems work can solve.

Take *Moby Dick* as an example and the author Herman Melville. The famous novel has been the subject of many movies and has thrilled millions of readers and viewers for years. The story is based on an actual event that happened in 1820, which became the subject of a movie released in 2015, way over a hundred years after Melville's death. In the story, a sailor named Ishmael narrates the obsessive quest of Captain Ahab, the captain out for revenge on Moby Dick, a great white whale, which on a previous voyage had destroyed Ahab's ship and ripped off his leg. *Moby Dick* is considered one of the great American novels of the 20th century. William Faulkner even confessed he wished he had written it himself and D. H. Lawrence called it one of the strangest and most wonderful books in the world.

"Call me Ishmael," is the first line of *Moby Dick,* the greatest book of the sea ever written—and one of literature's most famous opening sentences. Now that may sound like a resounding success after all these years, but it wasn't for the author. During Melville's life, the novel was a commercial failure and out of print at the time of his death in 1891. Only about 3,200 copies were sold during the author's lifetime, earning him just a little more than $1,200.

Like the great white whale that eluded Captain Ahab until finally killing the captain, the novel itself seemed to elude fame and fortune for the author. It took Melville a year and a half to write. He was so motivated by the real story, he became a crew member on a whaler. And some of Melville's real life experiences at sea became part of the novel, offering detailed and realistic descriptions of whale hunting and extracting whale oil as well as life aboard ship.

In the end, long after his death, we know that the end of the story is a success story, a great result of all the work that Melville put into it. The thing is, Herman Melville loved

Choosing and then completing the right work is key to achieving success.

to write. It was the writing itself, not the fame and wealth that was enough for him. Failures will not see that hard work alone is very much of a result. The hard work, even taking a job on a whaling ship to help write a story is not something that many would do.

If you give up before you have achieved your goal, it's either because you didn't want it badly enough to stay with it or you didn't realize that you could really have achieved it; you weren't sure. And as Shakespeare put it, "Our doubts are traitors and make us lose the good we often might win by fearing to attempt."

Decide what you really want. Make sure it's one thing, not two or more. Since it's only possible to get to one place at a time, make up your mind to pay the price that life asks for the accomplishment of it. If you do this, you'll definitely achieve what you set your heart upon.

Thoughts to Think About

1. What do you want more than
    anything else in the world?

2. If you answered wealth, are you willing to spend from
    12 to 18 hours a day for a number of years earning it?

3. What was the happiest, most joyful day of your life?
    Can you trace it back to a moment of giving, of sharing?

Notes:

_____

_____

_____

_____

_____

_____

_____

_____

_____

_____

_____

_____

_____

_____

8

SUCCESS'S COMMON DENOMINATOR

Distractions undermine even the best plans.

Successful people are influenced by the desire for pleasing *results*. The opposite are influenced by the desire for pleasing *activities*. They're inclined to be satisfied with what can be obtained by doing things they like to do.

Early in his or her career, the successful person forms the habit of planning days in advance, sticking to that plan if possible, and getting the greatest good out of every available hour. I'm certain you agree that this isn't as easy as it sounds. There are distractions that tend to undermine even the best plans. There's often something we'd rather do than our work. It seems natural to yield to these distractions, to allow ourselves to get wrapped up in some unproductive activity; but remember, success is unusual and not to be achieved by following our usual likes and dislikes. The hours we spend on the job are devoted to many different acts.

Successful people are influenced by the desire for expected results.

These acts can be grouped under one of two categories: 1) goal achieving or 2) tension relieving. Goal-achieving acts are usually productive. In sales work for example, prospecting, preparing for presentations, calling on clients and prospects, following up on sales and studying for self-improvement all come under this heading. Under the tension-relieving heading are frequent coffee breaks, long unproductive lunch hours, and unnecessary conversation with people who are not connected with our job.

Productive goal-achieving acts lead to beneficial results, while unproductive tension-relieving acts are merely superficial activities that do nothing to move us forward. Of course people need to relieve their tensions too at times. They need coffee and lunch, but one of the secrets of success is knowing how to keep our unproductive time to a minimum while concentrating on acts that are most productive and lead to positive results. We all know people who claim that a few hours a day is all they really need to complete their duties at work.

Well, obviously, they're mistaken and their mistake often costs them the success that could be theirs. There never has been, there is not now, and I don't believe there ever will be a time when a person can achieve anything outstanding by working only a few hours a day. Success doesn't come easily. It requires hard work and dedication and time.

Everyone has a tendency to waste time. Maybe it's because we don't realize that time is one of the few precious gifts we have. Every day and every year, everyone starts out with exactly the same amount of time. The way people make use of their time shows up in the results they achieve.

I have a neighbor who regularly spends quite a bit of time developing himself and his professional abilities. Where does he find that time? He finds a few minutes here,

The common denominator of success is forming the habit of making the wisest possible use of time, one act at a time all day long.

an hour there and 20 minutes somewhere else; and when he finds it, he asks himself, *How can I best use this time?* He takes every opportunity to learn more about his business and his career. He says it's as though he has the privilege of inviting into his mind the great authorities in any area he wants to explore, and these guests tell him how to get more out of living and more out of his work. Making choices like this, you couldn't pay my neighbor friend to go back to his old tension-relieving, time-wasting inactivity.

Time is available for us to use, it's up to us whether we make a habit of using it wisely. One of the easiest ways to form the habit of making a wise use of time is to think for just a moment before we begin a new activity. Pause and think. *Is this act productive, goal-achieving, or tension-relieving?* You might want to keep track to see how you're measuring up. Do this often enough, and the wise investment of time becomes a habit. The habit of acting in your own best interest.

The common denominator of success is forming the habit of making the wisest possible use of time, one act at a time all day long. Form this habit and you might just become one of the most competent people of your generation.

Thoughts to Think About

1. Are you easily distracted? What are the top three distractions that can quickly disrupt your focus?

2. For the majority of your day at work, are you focused on goal-achieving or tension-relieving acts?

3. The common denominator of success is forming the habit of making the wisest possible use of time, one act at a time all day long. Does this common denominator of success define your moment-by-moment lifestyle?

Notes:

_____

_____

_____

_____

_____

_____

_____

_____

_____

_____

_____

9

HUMAN DYNAMOS

The key to personal excitement and an enjoyable life is a great motivating desire.

Did you ever wonder where those human dynamos—those people who can pack as much work into one day as most of us do in two—get all the energy and drive that makes them go?

I believe that the source of drive and energy in human beings is known—it's the personal excitement that comes from a great motivating desire. If you ask most people why they get out of bed in the morning and slug away all day on the job, they'll probably have to think about it a while before coming up with an answer. When they do, it's usually along the lines of, "Oh, to pay the rent," or, "To put food on the table." Answers like these aren't exciting or motivating.

I belong to the human dynamo group that thinks life is far too short to be dull. Shelter and food we need; but unless we're living out in the street or starving to death, we're not too excited about a place to sleep or something to eat. Those who have no exciting reason to get out of bed in the morning may be fine people, but they never seem to accomplish much out of the ordinary—and they miss a lot of fun and a lot of rewards they could be enjoying.

The non-dynamos haven't the drive to become outstanding because they don't have a great motivating desire. The key that unlocks energy is desire. It's also the key to a long and interesting life. To expect someone to do something we want done, we have to get the person excited. Likewise, if we expect to create any drive, any real force within ourselves, we have to get excited. We have to decide upon something we desire very much. A goal that fires our imagination with a mental picture of having something, doing something, or being something.

Those who have no exciting reason to get out of bed in the morning miss a lot of fun and a lot of rewards they could be enjoying.

Fire Your Imagination

In a company we surveyed, we noticed that one of the men had won the admiration of all the others. He had thorough knowledge of the company, its products, markets, and competitors. He took pains to understand the customers and their problems. These things, along with an easy manner and a good personality, marked him as an outstanding employee.

When we asked him about all this, he said, "When I accepted a position with this company a few years back, I decided to shoot for a manager's job in one of our districts. I'm doing everything I can to be the kind of man who would have that job." That explained everything. In his mind, he was already running his own district. The rest of him was merely carrying out the motions that would soon propel him into the job he wanted.

Meanwhile, he was enjoying himself tremendously. The mental image of being a district manager so appealed to him that he found all the enthusiasm, energy, and drive he needed to achieve that position. Everything he said and did in his current job had to conform to the image he held in his mind. He was outstanding because nothing less than his best would fit with his goal. Of course he'll get that district manager's job and all that goes with it.

People with unusual drive and energy, people who excel are the ones who have given themselves a mental picture, a goal to work toward—and the amount of drive they possess will always be in exact proportion to the strength of their desire to make that mental picture a reality to reach that goal. We don't have to worry about setting a goal we can never reach. That's the strange and wonderful thing about humans, something that most people seem to miss. We never seriously desire anything we can't possibly have.

If you get all fired up over something, whether an executive position in your company, the income you feel you and your family need, or being someone who makes a real contribution by setting a fine example and helping others on their way up—if you can clearly envision how it will feel to satisfy your desire, then it can be yours.

Decide on the dream that's more important to you than any other, then begin to make that dream a reality.

You are a human dynamo full of potential!

The productive kind of desire is real. It's concrete. It's a mental picture that will never leave us alone. It's always there in front of our minds, prodding and poking, goading us on. It's an obsession, a whip. It has no mercy, and we'll never be satisfied until we've achieved what we truly desire.

How about you? What's your goal? What is it that gets you fired up every time you think about it? If you have such a goal, you'll never have to worry about the drive and energy you need to achieve it. But if you find that you lack drive, that you're short on energy, give it some thought; decide upon the dream that's more important to you than any other, then begin to make that dream a reality.

You will find that you have all the drive you need, all the energy you want to achieve your goals in life when you create a desire within yourself, then direct the energy and drive it generates toward getting whatever you want. You are a human dynamo full of potential!

It's been truthfully said, what the human mind can conceive and believe, it can achieve. There's an interesting fact that the average person tends to lose sight of or simply doesn't know, that we have the power and the energy to achieve what we want very much. Energy cannot be created in anyone, but understand that it's there within you.

A great and powerful sleeping giant is waiting to be awakened—and the waking agent is desire. Your desire to attain a worthy personal goal will unleash abundant energy for you. Then you will have all you need to travel an exciting, interesting, and fulfilling road through life to the destinations of your choice.

Thoughts to Think About

1. How about you? What's your goal? What gets you fired up every time you think about it?

2. Do you lack drive? Are you short on energy? Would setting a goal cause excitement and anticipation?

3. How ready are you to travel an exciting, interesting, and fulfilling road through life to the destinations of your choice?

Notes:

_____

_____

_____

_____

_____

_____

_____

_____

_____

_____

_____

_____

_____

10

CREATING A TIDAL WAVE OF SUCCESS

*All human activities are based
on the desire for increase.*

If our goal is high, our task will be harder—but not nearly as hard as the task that must be borne by those who make no decision at all. These are the people who bear the heaviest task. They might think they're avoiding responsibility by not setting a particular wage they want to receive from life. But they're the ones who must learn, to their dismay, that any wage they had asked of life, life would've paid.

The next time you get some free time, I encourage you to sit down with a pencil and paper and write down your current "wages." These should include not only financial wages but also the love and goodwill you receive from family and friends; your home, pets, and the benefits you receive from the world and life in general. Also, review the place where you now find yourself in relation to the goal you've established for yourself.

A friend of mine divides a paper down the middle with a line, and on one side he writes what he wants from life and on the other, the things he has so far; this way he keeps right on schedule. Just as a business must from time to time take inventory of its stock to find out where it stands, we should do the same. You too might want to get a piece of paper and draw a line down the middle, it's a lot of fun. Remember, wages are earned—and you reap what you sow.

Redistribution of Wealth

From time to time the debate over income redistribution comes up. There are certain truths that are true no matter how much the world may question or deny them. In the economic realm for instance, you can't legislate the poor into freedom by legislating the wealthy out of it. You can't multiply wealth by dividing it. Governments can't give to people what they don't first take away from people—which means one person receives without working, and another man works without receiving.

And nothing can kill the initiative of a people quicker than for half to get the idea they need not work because the other half will feed them. For then, the other half gets the idea it does no good to work since someone else receives the rewards of their labors. Closing our eyes to these facts

Initiative dies when people think they don't have to work.

will not change them. The quickest and surest way to lose a friend is to take care of him financially for a long period of time.

Some people confuse dependency with security, but it is nothing of the sort. Dependency makes us dislike ourselves. But rather than look at ourselves honestly and blame ourselves for our lack of courage, we blame the person (or government) we are dependent on. And it is clear that the more you give to someone who doesn't work for it, the more they take what you give for granted and as a result want more. It's so strange that these proven truths are never learned by the bulk of any given generation.

We can read of how the citizens of once free lands let their precious freedom slip through their fingers, and yet we can't see how history repeats itself. It will repeat itself, not because of the perversity of history, for history is nothing but the actions of men. We who shape the history of tomorrow must learn from the tragic mistakes of the past.

When we remove responsibility from the hands of the people and place it in the hands of government, freedom is ransomed. In seeking security through government controls, we lose all security since such a government cannot stand.

I think we should remember that the hardest life with freedom holds more hope, more joy, more satisfaction, and more opportunity in one day than a thousand years of soft living without it. The joy and excitement of accomplishment may be one of the best results you can ever hope to achieve. That being said, is there a way to up the odds in your favor? Maybe even guarantee your success? Yes!

Here are a few thoughts that you can make your own. Thoughts that if you do make them your own will guarantee your success all the years of your life. Now that's quite a statement, but it's true. Now to begin, let's understand that growth and increase are part of mankind and all of

The joy and excitement of accomplishment is one of the best results you can ever achieve.

Getting rich is getting whatever you want.

nature. It's inherent in each of us to desire more, this isn't wrong it's perfectly natural and the way it should be. This is true of all the members of our families, our friends and associates, our customers. You should want to get rich in every department of your life. But what do I mean by rich? Getting rich for you is getting what you want very much.

For some getting rich means a bigger income or a large sum of capital, and that's fine. You can get it without hurting or even competing with any other person. In fact, you can thereby increase the general well-being of everyone with whom you come in contact. No one can become rich in any way without serving others. Anyone who adds to prosperity must prosper in turn.

Getting rich for you may mean receiving more love, having greater peace of mind, owning the home of your dreams, or accomplishing something you've set your heart upon. In short, getting rich is getting whatever it is you want very much. It's as simple as that.

The first step in the process is to understand completely that it's right and okay for you to want what you want. All human activities are based on the desire for increase, people seeking more food, more clothes, more knowledge, more pleasure, more life. The next step is to understand that you need not compete with or deprive anyone.

Don't compete, create. In this way you add to the general well-being without taking anything away from anyone. Remember to give to every person more than you take. Now at first this may sound absurd, so let's dig into it a little. For a business or a person to expand—and remember, expansion is the natural desire of mankind—we must give more in use value than we charge. How much does it cost to give love, respect, and consideration to those near you? Very little, just a little extra effort. Yet love, respect, and consideration are priceless to the person receiving them.

This is the key, give more than you receive in everything you do. In this way you build a great credit for yourself that must come to you in some form sooner or later. You are putting in more goodwill than you're taking out and by so doing you're creating a tidal wave of future prosperity. This is the law of increase.

Give more than you receive in everything you do.

Thoughts to Think About

1. If your goal is high, your task will be harder—but not nearly as hard as the task of those who make no decision at all. They will learn that any wage they wanted would have been attainable. What do you think of those two statements?

2. What are your feelings about "redistribution of wealth"?

3. What specifically does getting rich mean to you?

Notes:

_____

_____

_____

_____

_____

_____

_____

_____

_____

_____

_____

_____

_____

_____

_____

_____

_____

_____

_____

_____

_____

_____

_____

_____

_____

_____

_____

_____

_____

_____

_____

_____

_____

_____

11

GROW YOUR TALENTS

*How can I best order my human resources
and apply them to my field of interest to
maximize my service to others? When
serving others with my talents, my
goals and desires will fall into place.*

Millions who find their lives boring, who find themselves depressed, at odds with themselves and others,
who find themselves suffering from a restless discontent—called the ill condition of our times—should seek
ways to be of service. No longer will they lead boring lives,
be depressed, or suffer from discontent. It's true. When
you are putting others first, your life becomes excitingly
content.

I read about a psychological test in which you're supposed to complete 20 statements beginning with the
words "I am." On a sheet of paper, you write down the
number one and behind it write "I am," then complete
the sentence. You might begin by writing, "I am a human

creature." Then on line two, you again begin the statement with "I am," and make another statement about yourself.

You do that 20 times; before you reach 20, you're making some pretty revealing comments. You're digging for information about yourself. You're doing what the Greek philosopher Socrates suggested we do when he said that "The unexamined life is not worth living."

If in case you're looking for a way to offer service to others, you now have a very interesting and viable method of finding a clue as to the field through which you can make the greatest possible contribution. And by so doing, you will reap the greatest possible rewards.

I believe that serving each other is the way to happiness and fulfillment. If you took away the people we serve, our lives would become meaningless. People have everything in the world we can possibly want, and they will gladly share it with us if we will serve them to their satisfaction. The real purpose of our journey through life is to find out how best we can serve.

"I am..."

Dig for the Truth

Dig for truth about yourself—don't dig a hole to bury your treasure. The following is a story about faithful servants to illustrate how to best use your resource, your treasure: the Parable of Talents.

Several thousand years ago, a "talent" was a measurement of weight. One talent was a large sum of money, considering a talent weighed between 80 and 100 pounds. Now imagine the value in today's gold or silver prices. If an ounce of gold trades for more than $1,000, one talent would be worth more than $1 million. And 2,000 years ago, it took many years to earn just one talent in silver or gold. This story tells of a wealthy man who was about to leave on a business trip, and not knowing when he would return he called together three servants.

He gave five talents to the first. The second servant received two, and the third servant only one. The first servant who received the five talents traded all five, and made another five, doubling his investment. That's a pretty good return. The one who had received two also gained two more, doubling his investment. But the third servant who received only one, dug a hole in the ground and buried the one and only talent to keep it safe and hidden. When the wealthy man returned, he praised the first two servants for doubling the value of their talents. He told them since they were faithful over a few things, he would make them the ruler over many things.

But for the third timid and cautious servant who buried his treasure, things didn't go so good. The wealthy man took the servant's talent away from him and gave it to the first who had doubled his investment to ten talents. The parable's lesson: for everyone who has, more will be given in abundance; but for those who don't have, more will be taken away.

The truth is, we're all creatures of growth. Simply hiding our treasures does no good for anyone. So what are you doing with the talents that have been given to you?

The late and distinguished Dr. Abraham H. Maslow put it this way in his book *The Farther Reaches of Human Nature:* "If you deliberately plan to be less than you are capable of being, then I warn you that you'll be deeply unhappy for the rest of your life. You will be evading your own capacities, your own possibilities." And let me add this, if you think you can succeed in a large way and play it safe at the same time, you are sadly mistaken. Success takes risk.

Success takes full commitment. You go out on the limb, so to speak, and take your chances alone. The warm, comfortable, huddling masses must be left behind, along with the old neighborhood and the small dreams.

Risk and success are at opposite ends of the same balancing beam. You cannot have one without the corresponding weight of the other. Risk ups the ante, raises the greens fee, and limits the membership—but it makes playing more fun, and you seldom have to wait in line anymore.

If you deliberately plan to be less than you are capable of being, then I warn you that you'll be deeply unhappy for the rest of your life. You will be evading your own capacities, your own possibilities.

You have been given a huge stash of talents. How you use them is up to you.

There's more opportunity hidden in your daily work than you could ever develop in a lifetime—if you only look long enough to find it. You may have never thought much about this, but *there's no such thing as a job that can't lead to greatness*. If you take the time and thought to become great at what you do, at what you now do, and where you are now, there is no limit to your rewards.

Unless we take the time, thought, and study to become outstanding at what we're now doing, why should we think we could become great at something else? Yet somehow it always looks easier to succeed in another person's line of work.

There's more opportunity hidden in your daily work than you can develop in a lifetime!

The better idea is to synchronize the experience you already have in what you're now doing to build a stairway to reach just about anything you and your family could possibly want. And in a surprisingly short time.

The law of economics tells us that our rewards in life will always be in exact proportion to our contributions. So, think about how can you increase your contribution to others in what you're now doing. Your rewards will come naturally.

Thoughts to Think About

1. Take time to complete the psychological test by completing the 20 statements beginning with the words "I am."

2. What did you learn about yourself by writing the 20 sentences describing what/who you are?

3. List 10 talents and resources you have as a person. Are you growing those attributes and skills or are they buried under a pile of timidity and fear of risk?

Notes:

_____

_____

_____

_____

_____

_____

_____

_____

_____

_____

_____

_____

_____

12

CARVING OUT YOUR OWN PATH

All the years of your life are determined by your contribution, your service to others.

Do you know why some people are paid $20,000 a week, while others are paid the minimum wage? There's an investment banker in Los Angeles who earns about $40 million a year. As far as is known, there's no limit on earnings. What would you like to earn? Your salary is not all there is to living by any means, far from it, but it does pay the bills. And if you earn an income in the upper 5 percent of the population, in that top 5 percent of the pyramid that the sun hits first as the earth does its daily rollover act, it's nice up there, and shooting for it will bring out the best of everything that is in you.

"When you're aiming for goal-oriented success, you'll do more for others' benefit, make greater contributions, give more to charities, and help more people succeed. So

A little discontent is a good thing, especially when it's discontent with ourselves.

how about it?" That's a talk I'd like to give to young people. Some may say that type of logic would stir discontent among the young, but I would reply that discontent is the greatest motivator of all, and it's responsible for every great advancement to humankind from running water and the inside toilet to the supermarket. A little discontent is a good thing, especially when it's discontent with ourselves.

An effective environment is an incalculably powerful force—for good or bad. For example, the deepest craving of young people is to be liked by their fellow students. Acceptance and esteem in the eyes of their contemporaries is their most focused desire, so they do what the other kids are doing, and the other kids do what everyone else is doing, and they all act like each other. They dress alike, they talk alike, they laugh at the same things—even when it isn't funny.

It's at this critical age when they begin to play follow the leader. No, that would be all right. Rather, they play follow the follower. Day after day, week after week, month after month, year after year, these young, wonderful, impressionable people conform to one another. They never ask themselves, *Where are these people leading me to? Are they even qualified to lead me? Why am I conforming to what they think, say, do? Is belonging to this group that important? Too important to me?*

And that's a subtle trap that affects almost everybody. If we don't break out of that trap, sooner or later we'll end in it. Millions, no billions do. It's astonishing how many adults never break out. We see them in their fifties and sixties still playing to the wrong crowd, still trying to be one of the boys.

There are two distinct steps we must take as we carve our unique path in life. *First,* we need to decide how much money we really want, the exact amount. Once this decision is made, the *second* step is to forget the money and concentrate on improving what we now do, until we've grown to the size that will fit and naturally earn the income we seek.

When we are fully qualified for the amount of money we decide to earn, we will soon earn it. We will also discover that with our new powers and abilities, it's not more

Don't follow the follower.

difficult, perhaps even less difficult, than what we're now doing for the money we're now earning.

Ask yourself, *How much money am I willing to earn?* Realizing that the amount I earn will be an exact proportion of my skills, the demand for what I do, and the difficulty of replacing me.

There are really three amounts of money people should decide upon:

- One, the yearly income we want to earn now or in the near future.

- Two, the amount of money we want to have in a savings and or investment account.

- And three, the amount of money we want as a retirement income, whether we ever retire from active work or not.

Here is where most people make a very serious mistake. They never decide on any of these three amounts of money. If you decide on these three amounts and write them on a card to carry with you or put somewhere where you can review it from time to time, you will automatically have placed yourself in that top 5 percent we were talking about. You have a plan for your future, a blueprint for future financial accomplishment. You know where you're going—and if you're serious about it, you most certainly will get there.

The trouble with people not achieving their goals is because they don't set any goals. They could most certainly reach their goals if they set them, if they seriously considered the goals they want to achieve. But they leave their future to chance, and find out sooner or later and to their sorrow, that chance doesn't work, that they've missed the boat.

It's estimated that only 5 percent decide on the amount of money they want to earn, and then grow as persons into the size of the incomes they seek. You must take your life, your fortune and your future into your own hands and accomplish your goals right on schedule all the years of your life. You can do it starting right now!

Write your list of goals. Carve your path to the future right now.

The Fundamental Basis of Future Success

A young person first starting out in the pursuit of a career, whether a college graduate or not, often begins on the wrong foot. In talking with many young men, I hear them say, "I want the job that pays the most money," and this is usually followed by the comment, "And offers the most security." As Clarence Randall, successful American business executive, advisor to US presidents, and author stated:

> The young man who reaches his big decision
> and chooses business as a career solely on the

basis of money, will live to regret it. When at long last he comes to the end of that career, he'll have nothing but money to show for it. He will have missed the deep satisfactions that will come to those of his classmates who make their decisions on the basis of how they might render the greatest service to the society that gave them their opportunity.

I'm certain a large percentage of young people entering the world of business might consider this pure nonsense, but Mr. Randall is right. But don't confuse rendering the greatest service to society with missing out on the money end of things. Those who find the way to render the greatest service can forget all about money. It'll take care of itself, and they'll often earn far more money in the long run than they would have if it had been their main consideration in the beginning.

Young people thinking of the future and trying to decide what to do with it should keep in mind the law of economics: Our rewards in life will be in exact proportion to our

Our rewards in life are in exact proportion to our contribution, our service to others.

contribution, our service. They should ask themselves, *How can I make the greatest contribution to society? I know some of my strengths and some of my weak points, and considering myself in total, what can I do to make the most of me and the best possible contribution to society?*

I think the words "contribution to society" frequently throw us off course. It sounds too much like saying "save the world," but it's actually quite simple. By putting money first and our natural aptitudes and real interest second, we may quite easily keep ourselves from the money we could have ultimately earned in a field where we would also have known the greatest satisfactions.

So as to a person's best interest as well as society's, if we make an earnest attempt to find the field in which we can make the greatest contribution, if we concentrate only on this and commit ourselves to what we have chosen, we need not think about the rewards. The rewards will certainly take care of themselves.

Choosing a lifetime career may be a difficult task, but if you are guided by the ultimate rule, "How can I make the greatest contribution to society?" your successful future is assured.

Thoughts to Think About

1. Have you ever been—or are you now—caught up in following the followers? Do you need to have a talk with yourself to the tune of, *Where are these people leading me to? Are they even qualified to lead me? Why am I conforming to what they think, say, or do? Is belonging to this group that important? Too important to me?*

2. Write the amounts you have chosen to carve into your future:

    - The yearly income I want to earn now or in the near future. $ _____

    - The amount of money I want to have in a savings and or investment account. $ _____

    - The amount of money I want as a retirement income, whether I ever retire from active work or not. $ _____

3. Have you asked yourself lately: *How can I make the greatest contribution to society? I know some of my strengths and some of my weak points, and considering myself in total, what can I do to make the most of me and the best possible contribution to society?*

Notes:

_____
_____
_____
_____
_____
_____
_____
_____
_____
_____
_____
_____
_____
_____
_____
_____
_____
_____
_____
_____
_____

_____

_____

_____

_____

_____

_____

_____

_____

_____

_____

_____

_____

_____

_____

_____

_____

_____

_____

_____

_____

_____

_____

13

HAPPY WITH YOURSELF?

What will really make you happy?

If you're not happy with yourself at this stage, perhaps it's time for a change. Get out your yellow pad again and write down the things you want. Don't worry about the order or what you list, just write each down as it comes to you. Big things, little things, things like income, or a certain sum you'd like to have working for you. Write down everything you want. This is your personal list—no one else has to see it.

After you've listed everything you want, chances are the list will be shorter than you would've believed before tackling it. After you're finished writing your list, number the items in the order of their importance to you—or in the order you want to achieve each one. On another piece of paper, write them in the proper order and toss the first sheet away.

Now you might think, *But isn't that rather selfish writing down everything I want? What good will that do for the rest of the human race?* I'll tell you right now, you will do more good for the human race when you enthusiastically go full bore after the things you want than in any other way—because the only way you can get the things you want is by providing service to others, and the more intense and enthusiastic you are about it, the better will be your service.

Provide What the Market Needs

This is the way the free market, private enterprise American system works. You will do and be your best when pursuing your personal goals. In so doing, you will provide the maximum service to those you want to help, and in turn help yourself. That's what's so hard to auger into the heads of the intellectuals who talk about a better distribution of income. There's certainly no secret about it, we do what we need to do to meet our serious needs and wants—and help others in the process. Don't wait for the right job to just come along—change your focus to what the market needs, then work toward providing it.

The company, industry, or government we work for are not responsible for our economic well-being. We as individuals are responsible for our economic well-being. If we work hard and conscientiously at our job with our eyes on a worthwhile goal in life, we'll achieve it and nothing can keep us from it. But if we act as if we're doing the company a favor by showing up every morning and doing no more than

If you work hard and conscientiously at your job with eyes on a worthwhile goal in life, you will achieve it.

enough to sneak by, sooner or later we will be terminated. There's just no doubt about it.

If you are looking for a job, figure out what you are bringing to the company. After you have decided what you have to offer, then start checking into what the company has to offer. Be certain that you can't receive more than you're giving. If someone expects a perpetual Christmas career, that person has simply never grown up intellectually or emotionally.

To make the best of a job, in fact, even making it fun and gaining a great future, make up your mind to become the best employee there is at your particular work. Also, you'll be amazed at how rapidly you move up the ladder, leaving behind those who think the world owes them a living. If you don't like your current income, it's best to take a long, searching look at your contribution. What are you doing in your job that no one else could do?

I know a man who is the head of one of the largest, best-known companies in the United States, yet he can hardly put 10 words together in their proper order. If murdering the English language were a misdemeanor, he'd be on death row. Yet he has mansions, yachts, private jets, the works.

With no more than perhaps a sixth grade education and the apparent determination to assiduously avoid any improvement to it, how has this man and his family enjoyed such spectacular financial success? Answer: He knows how to serve the people. His organization serves millions of people every day of the week. He worked hard all of his life

Be motivated to give the last ounce of yourself in the achievement of your goals.

to build the great organization he has, and he's done a fine job of it. So yes, he can pay cash for a $3 million yacht. And when he wants to go someplace in a hurry, his Gulf Stream 3 jetliner is warmed up and ready for him when his chauffeur takes him to the airport.

But most people in that top 5 percent have impeccable communication skills, are educated, are well-mannered, and are known for their character and integrity. Many of them are not rich by the standards of our mega-millionaire example, but they're in the top 5 percent of American incomes. They're set for life, and they as a group tend to enjoy themselves very much. They play a better game of golf or tennis than most of the country's hackers, they love their lifestyles, and they are happy with themselves.

You can be too!

Thoughts to Think About

1. "Free enterprise, or the free market, refers to an economy where the market determines prices, products, and services rather than the government. Businesses and services are free of government control." Put this definition into your own words. Do you believe this is the best economic system?

2. "Redistribution of income and wealth is the transfer of income and wealth (including physical property) from some individuals to others through government control and social mechanisms including taxation, welfare, public services, land reform, monetary policies, and confiscation." What are your thoughts about this economic system?

3. Influential and well-known political theorist John Locke said, "The state of nature has a law of nature to govern it, which obliges every one: and reason, which is that law, teaches all mankind, who will but consult it, that being all equal and independent, no one ought to harm another in his life, health, liberty, or possessions." How does this statement sync with the first two definitions of economic systems?

Notes:

_____
_____
_____
_____
_____
_____
_____
_____
_____
_____
_____
_____
_____
_____
_____
_____
_____
_____
_____
_____
_____
_____
_____
_____

14

GET RICH RISKS

*People don't get rich by accident,
they plan to get rich.*

Have you ever thought you might like to get rich? No, I'm not kidding. Usually, people don't get rich by accident, they plan it that way. I can tell you how to get rich; but from then on, of course, it's up to you.

Getting rich is a three-step process, and you don't have to worry much about competition because very few people will even try. It's a game any number can play. There's plenty of money around, more than enough for the few who will go to the trouble to enter the big game.

In the world of today, money is a nice to have. We tend to think of money not so much as a pile of cash, but rather in light of what it produces—a lovely home, college for the kids, travel, long vacations, a tailored wardrobe, financial independence, and security in our old age. No, there's nothing wrong with money, not a thing.

So if you want to get rich, know that "rich" is relative. For example, $20,000 a year would be riches to a lot of people; for others, rich would be a million dollars. Regardless of how much you need to be rich, the same system works.

Three Rules for Riches

Get out your pencil again and circle or underline the following three rules for getting rich. You can get started right away if you want to. Here they are:

Rule number one: Actually, this is the hardest rule of the three. The first rule is to *make up your mind that there's no good reason why you can't get the money you and your family want.* Your family may have been poor for as far back as you can trace your family tree, but it doesn't mean a thing. Remember that even with the wealthiest families in the world, way back somewhere, one person had to start the ball rolling. It all started with one poor individual with a good idea in every case. If other people can get rich, so can you. You have just as much on the ball and in many cases, probably a lot more than a lot of people who have nabbed the golden ring on life's merry-go-round. The largest industrial empire in the country was started by one person's idea. Every small business started that way too. You don't have to go into business for yourself to get rich—just make up your mind that you can do it. Rule number one is vital.

Rule number two: *Decide on the exact amount you want to earn and set a time limit for yourself.* Be realistic and sensible. Ask yourself what your qualifications are and set a reasonable amount of money in a reasonable length of time. Make up your mind at the same time that you're going to concentrate on these goals exclusively until you've reached both the amount and the timeframe.

Rule number three: The proven formula for financial success has never changed since the first coins were minted in Asia Minor. I can give it to you in six words, *find a need and fill it.* That's your part of the bargain. Nobody can lead a person by the hand to success. This is what the individual person must accomplish, and this is what makes it one of the most interesting games in the world—*find a need and fill it.* There's a lot more opportunity today than in our ancestors' day. The way to find the need is to look where you are right now. Don't go afar into strange areas where you have no experience.

Three Steps to Riches

In addition to three rules, I believe there are three steps to riches as well:

- **One,** make up your mind.
- **Two,** choose the amount you want.
- **Three,** find a need and fill it.

Easy? No, but it works.

How much money would you like to spend, say, every week? Nobody knows for sure who holds the record for spending the most money in the shortest time, but I can tell you who would be an excellent candidate, Ivar Kreuger. At least he'd rank up among the greatest swindlers in history. They called him the Swedish Match King. His criminal career began in 1922 when his Stockholm firm, Kreuger and Toll, started to expand its match manufacturing monopoly in Sweden. Within the following four years, the company had not only taken over more than 250 match factories in 40 countries, but also owned or controlled scores of other enterprises such as newspapers, mines, and telephone companies. Although many of these organizations were non-existent and many others were small and unprofitable, Kreuger produced glowing financial statements on them all and therefore was able to sell large issues of their stocks and bonds.

As Freling Foster tells it in his book, *Keep Up with the World,* as the capital of new companies was used to pay the interest and dividends of the others, Kreuger managed to expand his empire without arising suspicion. Moreover, he never allowed a business associate to become acquainted with more than one or two of its numerous ramifications. Finally, his financial structure became so big and complex that he was no longer able to handle it alone and consequently, realizing he would soon be exposed, in desperation he killed himself in Paris in March 1932.

The examination of his books and records, which took 30 investigators eight months to complete, disclosed that Kreuger had swindled investors out of more than $500 million, half of the amount having come from the United States. The report also disclosed that during the last 10 years of his life, Kreuger, although a bachelor, had maintained three country estates and homes in five cities and had personally spent, get this, an average of $180,000 a week. That's $9,360,000 a year, not that he earned but that he actually spent, which comes to $25,714 a day, seven days a week.

Now, friend, that's getting rid of money on a pretty fancy scale, of course, it wasn't his money. He had convinced so many reputable people that he was an honest businessman that when he saw that his enormous phony empire was about to crash down around him, he committed suicide. In all the stories I've read of famous swindlers and con men, I have yet to learn of one who didn't wind up in prison, committing suicide, or penniless, or a combination of two or all three. Sooner or later, the acts always fall.

Remember, a swindler's downfall is inevitable.

In recent times, we can consider the Ponzi scheme of Bernie Madoff, who defrauded thousands of investors out of tens of billions of dollars. He was just one of many people who took advantage of innocent people tapping into the gold lust that is both motivator and weakness. Madoff was sentenced for money laundering, securities fraud and other felonies and is said to be the most egregious conniver in history. The result of his decades-long scheme: $170 billion in restitution forfeiture and 150 years in prison, where he died at the age of 82.

The risk of losing everything and going to jail doesn't stop some people from trying to get rich illegally. The element of risk is not bad, but the means to the end needs serious analysis. There are risks in everything.

Have you ever given much thought to the idea that the spoils in life go to the risk takers? If you think about it, you may come up with the same solution as I. A survey indicated that 98 percent of the men in the country are looking for security in their work. That is, they're mainly interested in losing themselves deep in the warm, nourishing viscera of some large corporation, which is fine. I'm not knocking it, I'm just commenting on it.

These are not, as a rule, the risk takers, they're more the play-it-safers. And while they can have good and successful careers all their working lives, the chances are against them hitting the big jackpot. I say this because usually this sort of life does not encourage a person to do much more than he has to do, and he'll typically spend his free time—which comes to about 72 hours a week when neither working nor sleeping—pursuing things not calculated to help him get ahead in the world.

On the other hand, the person who risks their spare time writing a book, painting pictures, fiddling with inventions, and/or continuing his education, is generally the one who will advance above others. The person who risks all of his time on a goal he wants to reach, on a dream in his heart, who stakes his livelihood and the livelihood of his family on his own brains and the proper use of his time and tackles the world single-handed—here's the risk taker to whom the rewards will accrue.

Please know that I'm not talking about the impractical dreamer and stargazer. Rather, I'm talking about a person of action who gets out and raises the dust in the world. He might take some king-sized blunders and be snickered at by friends and relatives of a more conservative bent, but he will usually make the grade if he stays with it. And he earns their admiration, if not envy, before he is through.

One of the biggest factors in a risk taker's favor is the size of the group he belongs to. According to the most

Rewards will accumulate for the risk taker.

Unfortunately, humans tend to do no more than they have to do.

reliable figures I can find, risk takers belong to only about 2 percent of the population.

And since risk takers are generally working on an idea that will in some ways serve the big 98 percent, the odds swing rather favorably to his side. Additionally, someone on their own must devote more of their days to thinking.

Conversely, the person with a good, steady job, who's familiar with his work and surroundings can go along pretty well from day to day without doing any creative thinking at all. And as I've said previously, humans have a tendency to do no more than we have to do.

Anyone who spends a good deal of time thinking, will come up with a good idea once in a while. The law of averages is definitely on the thinker's side. And I'm sure you realize that it takes only a few, maybe only one really good idea to make it big.

The more you think about it and analyze it, the more you realize that what appears to be risky really isn't nearly as big a risk as you imagine. The cards are stacked pretty well for risk takers from several important standpoints. But as I said previously, the rewards definitely go to the risk taker. Life is full of hidden contradictions. One is that people who think they're playing it safe really aren't; and those who seem to take the greatest risks, considering the law of averages, are playing it safest.

Risks cannot be eliminated in your pursuit of purpose and the results you expect.

Thoughts to Think About

1. *Find a need and fill it.* Did an idea come immediately to mind when you read that directive? Or, was it immediately daunting to try and think of a need and how you could possibly fill it?

2. How ready are you to take these three steps today? Right now?

   - One, make up your mind.
   - Two, choose the amount you want.
   - Three, find a need and fill it.

3. On a scale from 1 (play-it-safer) to 10 (Evel Knievel), where are you as a financial or career risk taker? If not a 10, what would it take to move you toward a higher number on the scale?

Notes:

_____

_____

_____

_____

_____

_____

_____

_____

_____

_____

_____

_____

_____

_____

_____

_____

_____

_____

_____

_____

_____

_____

_____

_____

_____

_____

_____

_____

_____

_____

15

REAPING THE RESULTS
YOU WANT

*If you aren't in the process of getting
what you want, you probably don't know
what you want, have never defined
it, and aren't formulating a plan.*

To get the results you want, the following plan will help
you achieve your goals—*if* you follow it:

One, determine your objective. That is, make certain
exactly down to the last detail what it is you want to achieve
or obtain. Actually visualize it clearly in your mind, a mental
picture of the kind of person you want to be or whatever it
is you want very much.

Two, get the facts. Get all the facts about what is required
to attain the objective you've determined upon and visual-
ized. The more facts you can get, naturally the better.

Three, analyze, evaluate, and group these facts. Put them
in logical order of importance of accomplishment. In other

words, don't try to do everything at once. For example, a person who decided to become a brain surgeon wouldn't just start opening heads. His first job would be to qualify for a medical school. First things first. Ensure the goals are attainable and in order, and make certain they're practical.

Four, *set a timetable for the accomplishment of your objective*—then stick to it. Without a regular schedule to follow, people tend to put it off until some other time and finally wind up not doing anything about it.

Five, *have faith.* Have clear and abiding faith that you can achieve the objective you've set for yourself. Don't let anyone—friend, relative or foe—divert you from the way you've made up your mind to go.

Six, *take action today* to put your plan into effect. A plan without action is a futile dream. You'll never get to second base if you try to keep one foot on first. Take off.

Seven, *persistently take steps to further your plans.* Don't let obstacles get you down. Lots of circumstances might pop up to slow you down. They probably will. There are always obstacles in the way of anything worthwhile—but you can go around, over, or through them if you stay focused and goal-oriented.

Eight, *concentrate on one good step at a time* and don't try to walk in more than one direction at a time.

Nine, *regularly check up on yourself* and others assisting you on the way. Adjust your plans as required by situations you can't control. Study and follow your timetable.

Ten, *be sure to put your timetable on paper.* Don't try to keep the timing in your head. People who think that others get what they want in life because they're lucky are really wrong. Usually, these people are following a plan they have always had for the definite clear-cut goal they're working toward.

I remember when I was studying writing at school. My professor, one of the greatest who ever lived, said that a good story is one big event made up of a lot of little events along the way, but all leading to the one big event—and a successful life works out just about the same way!

You have just read the 10 points on how to get what you want. If you don't have or are not now in the process of getting what you really want, it's because you probably didn't know what you want, have never really defined it exactly or formulated a plan for its achievement.

Take this plan with 10 points seriously, and you will be on your way to achieving all that you want in life, and more.

Goal-oriented people follow their plan for the definite clear-cut goal they're working toward.

Thoughts to Think About

1. Which two of the 10 points made you want to take action immediately?

2. Which two of the 10 points made you want to push them way back to the far corner of your mind? In other words, ignore.

3. Which one of the 10 points will you begin taking action on today? Which one tomorrow? And so on? Write each step in order of your personal preference. Then take action.

Notes:

_____

_____

_____

_____

_____

_____

_____

_____

_____

_____

_____

16

SAILING ALONG

If you don't know where you're going, you won't get anywhere.

From time to time, I think every human being should ask themselves, *Am I sure I know the destination I'm sailing toward?* What point in time have I set as a target date for arrival? Am I currently on course to reach my destination?

Keeping track of your course is vital when navigating a boat, and your journey of living takes the same kind of navigation tracking. You need to chart a course from where you were or are, to the point you have decided to reach. Strange as it may seem, statistics indicate that the majority of people don't know where they're going in life, they have no destination in mind.

Most people don't know what they want to accomplish, what direction to go, when to arrive, and have no idea at all about such things. Anyone without a settled purpose, as Thomas Carlyle put it one time, is "like a ship without a rudder." This person is subject to every wind and tide, sailing

*Choosing a worthwhile goal
in life is the most important
decision you can make.*

first this way and then that way. If land should appear on the horizon, he wouldn't know what it is or where it is or whether or not it's worth sailing toward. What does he do? He merely exists.

And when the experts have questioned this individual, who makes up by far the great bulk of people in any country, he will usually answer that he is waiting. Waiting for something to happen, waiting for some "opportunity" to come along and carry him or her to some fine paradise on earth, some wonderful but totally unearned earthly nirvana where everything good will happen. It's a pity, really, that these people, and they're basically wonderful people, never quite get the word. They never seem to realize that if they don't know where they're going, they won't get anywhere. They don't seem to understand that a worthwhile goal in life is the most important decision a person can make.

Nor do they understand that if they would set a goal for themselves, they would in all likelihood achieve it. Far too many people take the attitude, although they would never admit it, that they've done enough by just being born and

You can sail successfully from one port to another all the days of your life and reap the rewards in joy of a life well lived.

that for the rest of their lives they should see how much they can get by doing as little as they possibly can.

No one has told them—and they will never or hardly ever discover it for themselves if no one does—that our rewards in life must and always will be an exact proportion to our service. And that by setting worthwhile goals in life, they can like the ships at sea, sail successfully from one port to another all the days of their lives and reap the rewards in joy of a life well spent.

Using Your Unconscious Mind

Humans have the ability to know what to do in complicated situations without being able to explain exactly how we know. This ability is found in our unconscious mind and enables us to perform enormously complicated tasks from reading and writing to composing music and inventing scientific theories. People who feel or intuit their way through these tasks actually have a competitive edge over those who consciously try to think their way through. This is not to say that an unconscious effort will always beat out a conscious one. A blending of the two modes of learning is still preferable to the use of only one or the other.

How many times have you heard yourself or someone else saying, "Darn, I should have followed my hunch!" That hunch, as we call it, is actually much more than that. It's the result of rich, deep intuitive powers based on millennia of successful adaptation to situations, and it's ready to lend its service instantaneously when we need an answer. It explains how we often know something without having any evidence to bolster our intuitive response. Our problems at such times often come from not listening to that inner voice and attempting to intellectually rationalize from apparent data, flimsy or convincing as it may be.

Ideas are the most important things on earth. Everything follows ideas. The idea must come first, good or bad, before something happens. We tell our grown children as they leave home to build lives of their own that they'll know what to do when faced with difficult situations, and they will. It will come from their teachings at home and formal education, and from their inner voices. Since we become

Think about beneficial ideas to meet your needs and wants, and the needs and wants of others.

what we think about, what we think about takes on new importance. We want to think about ideas that will prove beneficial to our needs and wants and to the needs and wants of others.

William Lyon Phelps, former president of Yale University, said that the most interesting people are those with the most interesting pictures in their minds. I agree. The ideas we hold direct the course of our lives; they are the pictures in our minds, our art gallery we might say. And our facial appearance after age 40, interestingly enough, is usually a reflection of that art gallery. We're told that our faces after 40 are our own responsibility. It's only natural that they will mirror the pictures in our minds.

Many people fail to put together a gallery of ideas that reflects good cheer, happiness, and hopeful expectation. I rather imagine that few people realize the importance of ideas in our lives, yet ideas are simply everything. And that's why living as a simple reflection of our neighbors and neighborhood isn't necessarily a good idea. It's the ideas we ourselves have considered and accepted as worthy of hanging in our mental gallery that determine the kind of persons we are.

Think of this: "I slept and dreamt that life was joy. I awoke and saw that life was service. I acted and behold, service was joy." Now there's an idea from which I derive a great deal of inner peace and contentment. No doubt when the great poet Rabindranath Tagore of Calcutta, India, worked that poem out, it was the exposure of an idea that meant a great deal to him. Joy, one of the greatest of life's treasures, comes from fulfilling our duty to those we've chosen to serve.

In the United States, we choose our work. It isn't forced upon us once we're independent adults. Doing it to the very best of our ability should bring us joy. If it doesn't, there's something wrong and it's very probably that we're in the wrong career or fail to see our work in the proper light.

Joy, one of the greatest of life's treasures, comes from fulfilling our service to those we've chosen to serve.

Thoughts to Think About

1. Ask and answer yourself: *Am I sure I know the destination I'm sailing toward? What point in time have I set as a target date for arrival? Am I currently on course to reach my destination?*

2. Has anyone told you or have you discovered for yourself that your rewards in life must and always will be in exact proportion to your service? Put that fact into your own words, reflecting your personal experiences of it.

3. What ideas have you considered and accepted as worthy of hanging in your mental gallery that have determined the kind of person you are? List them here.

Notes:

_____

_____

_____

_____

_____

_____

_____

_____

17

OPPORTUNITIES TO LAST A LIFETIME

You can alter your life by altering your attitude.

Again, I implore you to sit down to a clean sheet of paper. At the top of the paper, write your financial goal—the amount of money per year you intend to earn soon. Incidentally, you might like to keep this to yourself. It's nobody's business but yours.

Then start to think. Think about your goal and what it will mean to you and your family. Then see how many ideas you can come up with to help you reach that goal. Ideas to improve what you now do for a living and ways of increasing your contribution to match your income goal.

Jobs don't have futures, people do. No matter what line of work you may be in, there is within it more than enough opportunity to last a lifetime. You don't have to think of brand-new ideas or revolutionary new ways of doing things, although you well might come up with some.

Jobs don't have futures, people do.

Think of ways of improving what is now being done. If you're to increase your income by the amount you've specified, you must find ways of increasing your contribution, your service—and the key to this is to be found in your mind, in that gold mine between your ears.

Try for five ideas every morning, and write them down. Save those sheets of paper in a special "idea" file. Many, perhaps most, of your ideas will be worthless, but some of them will be very good. A few will be excellent, and every once in a while you will come up with something really outstanding. Five ideas a day is 25 a week, if you don't think on weekends, which is more than a thousand ideas a year! It takes only one idea to get you to that income you're shooting for. The law of averages swings so far in your favor you just can't miss.

Expectancy

Try to develop a sense of expectancy. That is, try to hold the feeling that the goal you're shooting for is a sure thing and that it's only a matter of time before it's realized. Henry

Ford didn't start making cars until he was 45 years old. A friend of mine started a new company at 65, and his new company has sales of better than $300 million a year. It's almost never too late.

Try not to think of things outside your own line of work or whatever it is you're most interested in. To think well and profitably, you must discipline your thinking. Keep it on course, controlled. Keep it in one field, specialize.

Attitude

Attitude has been called the most important word in the language. William James put it this way, "The greatest discovery of my generation is that human beings can alter their lives by altering their attitudes of mind." This statement is definitely something to think about. You can alter your life by altering your attitudes—which is another way of saying we become what we think about.

Look at it this way. Your total environment, if you've been an adult for any appreciable period of time, is a reflection of you as a person. The house and the neighborhood in which you live, the car you drive, the clothes you wear, your job, and the people with whom you regularly associate. Your total environment is an exact and merciless mirror of you as a human being.

If you feel your environment can stand some improvement, you have only to improve your attitude and your world will gradually change to reflect the changing person. Here's how to change your attitude. Beginning now, act as the person you most want to become.

Becoming

For example, if you already are certain of the goal you're shooting for, how would you conduct yourself in every situation? Well, conduct yourself that way now and tomorrow and the next day. Begin now to act the part of the person you most want to become and you'll end by becoming that person, subtly in little ways. In the way you dress, in the way you talk, in the unfailing courtesy you show to every person with whom you come in contact.

Begin to act the part of the person who has already achieved what you are aiming for. The German philosopher Goethe gave us the secret when he said, "Before you can do something, you must first be something." When you behave like the person you most want to become, the things that person would have will tend to come to you. It's simply cause and effect.

Always be suspicious of get-rich-quick schemes or sudden success.

Caution: Don't be in too big a hurry. It takes longer to build a skyscraper than a chicken coop. Build slowly, steadily, and well. Then when you make it, you'll keep it. You'll stay on top. Always be suspicious of get-rich-quick schemes or sudden success. Never forget the word "attitude." Your attitude toward the people you come in contact with determines their attitudes toward you.

The person with a great attitude toward life and the world is the person other people call lucky. He's not lucky. He's just using our friend, "cause and effect." His causes are excellent, and his effects have to be just as good. And that's it, simply.

Three things to remember, to practice every day: expectancy, attitude, become. If you spend 16 hours a day, seven days a week practicing your golf swing, in a relatively short time you will have a grooved, beautiful swing like the pros.

So to become the successful person you want to become, practice your hopeful expectancy, your new attitude, and act the part every day, every waking hour. Practice thinking a few minutes every morning and you'll find yourself thinking all day long. And always remember the formula—your rewards in life will always be in exact proportion to your contribution, your service.

Go over the ideas in this chapter every day until there are as much a part of you as your name and your temporary address. You'll notice that each time you read, you will learn something new. You will get a new idea you may have missed the first time around.

With a great attitude
you can succeed
with very little else.

Attitude comes very close to being everything about success or failure. With a great attitude a person can succeed with very little else. Attitude makes the sale or loses it. What is attitude? The dictionary describes it as a matter of bearing or mood, but it's much more than that.

Attitude is what sets the stage for what we want or expect to happen. The person who goes through life, as millions do, saying begrudgingly, "With my luck, the whole thing will go down in flames," over and over and over and over again. This person's attitude sets the stage for failure. This person expects failure, thinks about failing, and consequently fails over and over and over and over again. People can have a great education but with a bad attitude they will generally fail.

The attitude of excellence always results in excellence. You and I can see to it that we maintain an attitude of great expectations. It's more fun and so much more interesting to adopt and keep such an attitude, and it results in new levels of achievement.

A Drive for Excellence

We're not born with a drive for excellence in our lives and work. Those are uniquely human qualities that come from learning or experience or both. But we *are* born with exuberance and curiosity, and when these qualities are combined with great expectations, we can expect marvelous results! We try harder, we put more of ourselves into what we do when we have an attitude of great expectations. "That's good enough," won't do. Not for a moment.

I remember reading about Sir Henry Royce whose habit it was to stalk about the Rolls-Royce factory. One day he overheard one of his engineers saying to a worker, "That's good enough." He immediately broke into the conversation by shouting, "It's never good enough. That's what we're all here for, to make it better and then to make it better than it is today and then better than it is tomorrow. Never say it's good enough, it isn't," or words to that effect.

That's what the goal of excellence is all about.

Thoughts to Think About

1. Why do you think the author asks you to write down your goals—over and over? What is his reasoning for this repetition?

2. Will you take up the challenge to write down five ideas each day? Yes? No? Why or why not?

3. Would you say that on average you have a great attitude about life? A good attitude? A bad attitude? What would your family say about your attitude? How about your friends and coworkers?

Notes:

_____

_____

_____

_____

_____

_____

_____

_____

_____

_____

_____

18

DESIRE AND ENERGY EQUALS SYNERGY

The more people know, the more they realize their potential, the more enlarged their horizons.

A main issue of industry is motivating people. A company wants to motivate its employees to do really good work, to know the pride that comes from doing work well. Business wants to motivate its sales force to do a better job of selling and to motivate the consumer to buy the products it manufactures or the service it sells. Motivation is a key word.

I have long held the belief, and I'm sure I'm not alone, that the most effective means of motivating employees is through education, knowledge. It is obvious that the more a person knows, the more he comes to realize his potentialities, the more his horizons are enlarged. We know, for example, that energy is linked to desire. You will never find one without the other. The smaller a person's desire, the

People with the greatest desires always have the most energy.

smaller his or her energy. People with the greatest desires always have the most energy, which creates synergy that causes cooperation and productive interactions.

Exposing employees to greater knowledge increases their desires, and along with it, their energy, and along with that their production. A company that offers education is being anything but selfish. True, the company will benefit substantially and so will the consumer in that the product can possibly be produced for less money and the savings passed along to the customer.

This is the kind of benefit that has been earned through intelligently helping the employees who want a lovely home, a nice car or two, and a healthy savings account. This is not acquisitiveness, it is merely the normal and natural desire for a good life for ourselves and our children, and these things are possible for practically everyone in this country.

I think more people should be made to realize that the limitations they find in their lives are largely self-imposed and can usually be traced to a lack of information, a lack of knowledge. The more knowledge, the more people want;

the more they want, the harder they work; and the harder they work, the more they get.

The trouble with this picture, though, is the attempt to get more money, more leisure, more benefits for doing less work. While this sounds good, it simply isn't. Somebody has to pay the bill, and if the employee isn't willing to do it through a conscientious and intelligent attitude toward his job, the customer has to pay for it and the employee is the customer.

Now here's something worth remembering—it is impossible to get rich without enriching others. Whoever adds to prosperity must prosper in turn, this is always the way the ball bounces. And all attempts to sidestep this simple but all-powerful rule will end only in disappointment and frustration. I think if this information were made available in an effective manner to all young people beginning their working careers and to all those who find themselves with high pay but less work, during a year's time it would make sense to them. I think they would then realize the truth of the saying—*it is impossible to get something for nothing.*

It is impossible to get rich without enriching others.

Thoughts to Think About

1. Would taking the initiative to learn more about your field of endeavor be a benefit for you? How willing are you to take a night class or enroll in an online course?

2. How motivated are you to put more desire and energy into your current position, to work toward synergy with your leaders and colleagues?

3. Do the managers where you work hold employees accountable for trying to get more while doing less? Under what circumstances would you agree to do more than you're getting paid for doing?

Notes:

_____

_____

_____

_____

_____

_____

_____

_____

_____

_____

19

A 30-DAY EXPERIMENT

*Be of service, build, work, dream,
create. Do this and you'll find
there's no limit to the prosperity and
abundance that will come to you.*

I've explained the strangest secret in the world and how it works, now I want to explain how you can prove to yourself the enormous returns possible in your own life by putting this secret to a practical test. I want you to take a test that lasts for 30 days. It isn't going to be easy, but *if you give it a good try, it will completely change your life for the better.*

Sir Isaac Newton, the English mathematician, a natural philosopher, gave us some natural laws of physics that apply as much to human beings as to the movement of bodies in the universe. One of these laws is that for every action there is an equal and opposite reaction. Simply stated as it applies to you and me—we can achieve nothing without paying the price. The results of your 30-day experiment will be in direct proportion to your effort.

You can achieve every goal by paying the price in effort.

To be a doctor you must pay the price of long years of difficult study. And remember that each of us succeeds to the extent of our ability to sell. Selling our families on our ideas, selling education in schools, selling our children on the advantages of living a good and honest life, selling our associates and employees on the importance of being exceptional people. But to be successful in selling our way to the good life, we must be willing to pay the price. What is that price? The price is many things:

First, *the price is understanding emotionally as well as intellectually that you literally become what you think about. That you must control your thoughts to control your life. It's understanding fully that as you sow so shall you reap.*

Second, *the price is cutting away all shackles from your mind and permitting it to soar as it was divinely designed to do. It's the realization that your limitations are self-imposed and that the opportunities for you today are enormous beyond belief. It's rising above narrow-minded pettiness and prejudice.*

Third, *the price is using all your courage to force yourself to set a definite and clearly defined goal for yourself. To let* your marvelous mind think about your goal from all possible angles. To let your imagination speculate freely on many different possible solutions. To refuse to believe that there are any circumstances sufficiently strong enough to defeat you in the accomplishment of your purpose. To act promptly and decisively when your course is clear. And to keep constantly aware of the fact that you are, at this moment, standing in the middle of your own "acres of diamonds," as Russell Conwell pointed out.

Fourth, *the price is to save at least 10 percent of every dollar you earn.* It's also remembering that no matter what your present job it has enormous possibilities if you're willing to pay.

Now let's go over the important points and the price each of us must pay to achieve the wonderful life that can be ours. It is, of course, worth any price.

1. You become what you think about.

2. Remember the word "imagination" and let your mind begin to soar.

3. Courage. Concentrate on your goal every day.

4. Save 10 percent of what you earn.

5. Take action. Ideas are worthless unless we act on them.

Keep in mind that you have nothing to lose by taking this test, and everything you could possibly want to gain. There are two things that may be said of everyone: 1) Each of us wants something and 2) each of us is afraid of something.

I want you to write on a card what it is you want more than anything else. It may be more money, perhaps you'd like to double your income or make a specific amount of money. It may be a beautiful home, it may be success at your job, it may be a particular position in life. It could be a more harmonious family. Each of us wants something.

Now write down on your card *specifically* what you want. Make sure it's a single goal that is clearly defined. You needn't show it to anyone, but carry it with you so you can look at it several times a day. Think about it in a cheerful, relaxed, positive way each morning when you get up— and immediately you have something to work for, something to get out of bed for, something to live for.

Look at it every chance you get during the day and just before going to bed at night, remembering that you must become what you think about. And since you're thinking about your goal, you realize that soon it will be yours. In fact, it's really yours the moment you write it down and begin to think about it. Look at the abundance all around

Look at the abundance all around you—it's yours for the asking.

you as you go about your daily business. You have as much right to this abundance as any other living creature—it's yours for the asking.

New Habits

Now we come to the difficult part. Difficult because it means the formation of what is probably a brand-new habit, and new habits are not easily formed. Once formed, however, each will follow you the rest of your life. **Stop thinking about what you fear.** Each time a fearful or negative thought comes into your consciousness, replace it with a mental picture of your positive and worthwhile goal.

Don't give up. There may be times when you want to give up, as it's easier for a human being to think negatively than positively; that's why only 5 percent are successful. You must begin now to place yourself in that 5 percent group.

For 30 days you must take control of your mind. Only think about your goal and your journey to accomplish that goal.

Each day, for this 30-day test, **do more than you have to do.** In addition to maintaining a cheerful, positive outlook, give yourself more to do than you've ever done before. Do this knowing that your returns in life must be in direct proportion to what you give.

The moment you decide on a goal to work toward, you're immediately a successful person. You are then in that rare and successful category of people who know where they're going. Out of every 100 people, you belong to the top five. Don't concern yourself too much with how you're going to achieve your goal, leave that completely to a power greater than yourself. All you have to do is know where you're going. The answers will come to you of their own accord and at the right time.

Remember well the words of wisdom from the Sermon on the Mount. Keep them constantly before you this month of your test: *"Ask, and it will be given to you; seek, and you will find; knock, and it will be opened to you. For everyone who asks receives, and he who seeks finds, and to him who knocks it will be opened"* (Matthew 7:7-8 NKJV). A successful life is as marvelous and as simple as that. In fact, it's so simple that in our seemingly complicated world, it's difficult for an adult to understand that all we need is a purpose and faith. For 30 days, do your very best.

Go at your work with a calm, cheerful assurance *that time well spent will give you the abundance in return you deserve and want.* If you're a stay-at-home mom, devote your 30-day test to completely giving of yourself without thinking about receiving anything in return, and you'll be amazed at the difference it makes in your life. For 30 days, no matter what your job, do it as you've never done it before. And if you've kept your goal before you every day, you'll wonder and marvel at this new life you're creating.

Words to Live By

And don't forget the card, which is vitally important as you begin this new way of living to focus on your goal. On one side of the card is your goal, whatever it may be. On the other side write the words quoted from the Sermon on the Mount.

In your spare time, during your test period, **read inspirational books** including: the Bible, Dorothea Brande's *Wake Up and Live!*, *The Magic of Believing* by Claude Bristol, *Think and Grow Rich* by Napoleon Hill, and other books that instruct and inspire. Nothing great was ever accomplished without inspiration. See that during these crucial first 30 days, your own inspiration is kept high and energized.

And above all, **don't worry**—*worry brings fear and fear is crippling*. The only thing that can cause you to worry during your test is trying to do it all yourself. Know that all you have to do is hold your goal before you, everything else will take care of itself. Remember also to **keep calm and cheerful,** *don't let petty things annoy you and get you off course*.

Because this test is difficult, some will say, "Why should I bother?" Well, look at the alternative. No one wants to be a failure, no one really wants to be a mediocre individual, no one wants a life constantly filled with worry and fear and frustration. Therefore, remember that you always reap what you sow. If you sow negative thoughts, your life will be filled with negative things. If you sow positive thoughts, your life will be cheerful, successful, and positive.

Gradually you may forget what you've read here. I encourage you to read it often and keep reminding yourself what you must do to form these new habits. Gather your whole family around at regular intervals and talk about what you've read.

Service and Success

Success is not the result of making money—making money is the result of success, and success is in direct proportion to your service. Most people have this law backward. They believe that someone is successful if they earn a lot of money. The truth is that you can only earn money *after* you're successful.

It's like if someone sat in front of the stove and said to it, "Give me heat, and then I'll add the wood." How many men and women do you know or do you suppose there are today who take the same attitude toward life? There are millions. No. We have to put the fuel in before we can expect heat.

You can only get rich by enriching others.

Likewise, we have to be of service first before we can expect money. Don't concern yourself with the money. Be of service, build, work, dream, create. Do this and you'll find there's no limit to the prosperity and abundance that will come to you. Prosperity is founded upon a law of mutual exchange. Any person who contributes to prosperity must prosper in turn himself.

Sometimes the return will not come from those you serve, but it must come to you from someplace because that's the law. For every action there is an equal and opposite reaction. As you go daily through your 30-day test period, remember that your success will always be measured by the quality and quantity of service you render, and money is a yardstick for measuring this service. No one can get rich unless they enrich others.

Complete Then Repeat

Complete your 30-day test, then repeat, and then repeat it again—and each time it becomes such a part of you that you'll wonder how you could ever have lived any other way. Live this new way and the floodgates of abundance will open and pour over you more riches than you may have dreamed existed. Money, yes, lots of it.

But what's more important is the peace you have. You will be in that wonderful minority who lead calm, cheerful, successful lives.

Start today. You have nothing to lose and a lifetime of success to win.

Thoughts to Think About

1. To be successful, are you motivated
   to pay the price of:

   - Understanding emotionally as well
     as intellectually that you literally
     become what you think about?

   - Cutting away all shackles from your
     mind and permitting it to soar as it
     was divinely designed to do?

   - Using all your courage to force yourself to set a
     definite and clearly defined goal for yourself?

   - Saving at least 10 percent of
     every dollar you earn?

   - Taking action on your ideas?

2. Did you write the words of wisdom from the
   Sermon on the Mount on the back of your
   goal card yet? How will these words affect
   your life, your mindset, your future?

3. How comfortable are you discussing what
   you've read in this book with your family and
   friends? Would they, or do they, understand the
   process, concepts, and proven strategies?

Notes:

_____

_____

_____

_____

_____

_____

_____

_____

_____

_____

_____

_____

_____

_____

_____

_____

_____

_____

_____

_____

_____

_____

20

THE ODDS

The chances of failure are virtually nonexistent.

Now that you've reached the last chapter, you may be wondering, *What are the odds that someone who follows the guidelines in this book will actually succeed?* I confidently answer that the chances of failure are virtually nonexistent for anyone who seriously read and took to heart all the wisdom shared throughout each chapter. The odds of success are overwhelmingly in every reader's favor. In fact, there's nothing but success for the goal-oriented person.

If the reader is a river person, that individual automatically is a success as long as he or she is in the river. Remember the comment that Americans can become anything they want to become? The trouble is they seldom make the decision to become anything other than what they are.

Do you remember what Willie Loman said in Arthur Miller's great play, *Death of a Salesman*? He said, "The important thing is to be liked." Willie Loman never grew up.

Nothing but success.

He never knew who he was. His story is a modern tragedy, it's always been a tragedy. It's the story of the mob. When a person has no identity of his or her own, that person will seek to find identity in a larger group.

That's why joining groups of various kinds is so popular. In that way, we get a badge, a label that tells us what we are. Now we're properly labeled. This is not to say that successful men and women do not belong to organizations; they certainly do and they make major contributions to their organizations, but they don't need the organization for identity. They're quite aware of who and what they are; and if their organizations didn't exist, they would be successful independent performers in society. They would never feel lost.

Successful people follow independent paths. This is the important point to remember. At some point in their lives, they break away from the crowd and start on a path of their own. That's the adult, the intelligent thing for a human being to do. In striking off on an independent path, they're not necessarily alone, it's just that they join a much smaller group of like-minded people. They can't take the whole crowd into that top 5 percent.

The ancient Romans had their circus. Modern Americans have their television, which is far superior to the old Roman circus as they don't even have to leave the comfort of their living rooms to watch. It's true that there are many wonderful things on television, but millions of families watch TV all day, they're mesmerized by it. Yet when you think of all the productive and constructive things they could be doing instead, it's mind-boggling.

One of the best things about getting in that top 5 percent is that as we get older, life need not become less interesting for us or more laborious. We become more productive as we approach our 60s and 70s and often many years beyond—and it's nice to grow older with all the goodies of life. It's more comfortable. We can spend winters in Florida, or travel to places where the summers are cooler and the winters warmer or live in healthier climates where we can enjoy all the benefits of the good life.

But perhaps most importantly of all, we can say, "I gave it my best and I'm not through yet. It's been a wonderful

I gave it my best and I'm not through yet.

experience this holiday on earth, and I've enjoyed it very, very much. Now let's see what we can do with the rest of it."

Yes, I think it's actually easier to be goal-oriented. There's less competition up there where the view is so much better and the air is so fresh and clean; and it's almost never too late, for with a purpose, a worthy goal, and the motivation to reach those upper layers on the pyramid, a person can travel farther in a few years than he or she might otherwise travel in a lifetime.

Excuses and Alibis

I think one of the reasons you see so many angry drivers and glum, surly expressions on people's faces is because they're giving the world an alibi but can't fool themselves with it. Human beings will go to any length to keep from blaming themselves for their current, less-than-ideal situation. They say they came from the wrong side of the tracks, or never had a chance, or didn't get the breaks, or had to put their brother through school, or they have asthma. Any one of a thousand alibis to keep from telling the truth, to keep from saying, "I'm in this situation because of my own mistakes and my own foolishness."

Now here's where the real danger of an alibi comes into place. Once we start using an alibi, we're stuck with it. We have to keep using it to keep from admitting we were lying

Well, I've been something of a nitwit, but now I'm going to start over.

to ourselves and to everyone else—and as long as we hang on to an alibi, we're stuck. There's no synchronicity to work with to achieve success.

We must admit the truth, saying something such as, "Well, I've been something of a nitwit, but at least I finally recognize that fact and now I'm going to start over on the right foot." It's almost never too late if we're truthful to ourselves. As Shakespeare, put it, "To thine own self be true, and it must follow, as the night the day, thou canst not then be false to any man."

From the beginning, the best starting point for anyone's philosophy is Socrates' brief but powerful statement, "Know thyself." Because if you step out on the wrong foot, so to speak, you will stay out of step until you wake up to the fact that alibis don't make you look better in other people's eyes. But what's more important, you look smaller in your own eyes.

If you've been standing in your own light, hiding behind or under some moth-eaten, worn-out alibi because you've been too timid to stand up straight and do what you know you should be doing, if you've kept pushing down the truth that will get you on the road to greater things, right now is the best time to put that excuse under the bright, clear light of reason. No doubt it will disappear and you can breathe easy again—and set your sail in the direction of success!

Thoughts to Think About

1. What would you say your odds are for attaining success now that you've finished this book?

2. How much of your success is your responsibility to make happen?

3. What first comes to mind out of all that you've read as *the* most important piece of advice or tactic?

Notes:

_____

_____

_____

_____

_____

_____

_____

_____

_____

_____

_____

_____

_____

_____

_____

_____

_____

_____

_____

_____

_____

_____

_____

_____

_____

_____

_____

_____

_____

_____

_____

_____

_____

_____

_____

_____

ABOUT EARL NIGHTINGALE

Earl Nightingale (1921-1989) was a man of many talents and interests—nationally syndicated radio personality, entrepreneur, philosopher, US Marine, and more. One thread united all his pursuits—a passion for excellence and living a meaningful existence.

Earl Nightingale's life began simply. He grew up in Long Beach, California. His parents had little money, and his father disappeared when he was 12. But even as a boy, Earl was always asking questions, always reading books in the local public library, wanting to understand the way life works.

Stationed aboard the battleship USS Arizona, Earl Nightingale was one of a handful of survivors when that ship was destroyed and sank at Pearl Harbor. After being separated from the Marine Corps and starting with practically nothing, over the next ten years he founded and headed four corporations. In addition, he wrote, sold, and produced fifteen radio and television programs per week.

Nightingale appeared on all major radio networks. For four years he was the star of the dramatic series *Sky King,* which was carried on more than 500 stations of the Mutual Radio Network. He also began an insurance agency, and in twelve months led it from last to sixth place in the nation with one of the world's largest companies.

The Nation's Press carried the astounding story of the phenomenally successful young man who, at 35, had become financially independent. He produced his famous recording of *The Strangest Secret,* revealing how anyone can make the most of his or her own capabilities and can attain a rich full measure of success and happiness, right in his or her present job or position. Its theme: "How to achieve greater success and enjoy greater happiness and peace of mind."

At the time, this inspiring recording broke sales records, selling in the multimillions to major industries, retailers and salespeople, clubs and associations, parents, students, and people in virtually all walks of life. His masterful recording has been adapted into books and videos.

THANK YOU FOR READING THIS BOOK!

If you found any of the information helpful, please take a few minutes and leave a review on the bookselling platform of your choice.

BONUS GIFT!

Don't forget to sign up to try our newsletter and grab your free personal development ebook here:

soundwisdom.com/classics

ALSO IN THE
STRANGEST SECRET
SERIES

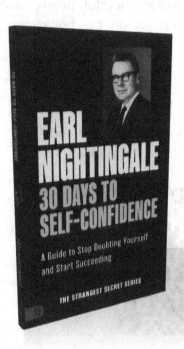

AVAILABLE EVERYWHERE BOOKS ARE SOLD
WWW.SOUNDWISDOM.COM